As I Took My Walk With God

Volume II: Greatness Was Upon Them

Jeremiah Short

ISBN: 978-0-9846412-7-7

Printed in the United States of America

Foreword by Dr. Steve Bezner

Cover Design by Mack L. Bishop III

This book is dedicated to Ms.Dixon for helping me realize what .
And my kids for allowing me to lead them to Greatness.

The Journey

Foreword

The Christian journey is just that--a journey. Those who decide to follow Jesus soon discover that following the Son of God is not something that magically moves one into immediate perfection or maturity.

In fact, those who follow Jesus discover that just as humans are always changing and growing, the spiritual journey is one of continual growth and change, as well.

For reasons that we do not immediately comprehend or understand, Jesus enjoys us growing and changing and He often uses painful experiences for our own benefit.

As I've watched Jeremiah over the last several years, it's his walking through painful and difficult circumstances that has, to me, been the greatest evidence of what God is doing in His life.

He is honest about his feelings in these situations. He admits that they are difficult to understand, to navigate. He confesses that he is often frustrated or angry. He admits when he is confused or unsure about what the outcomes of his actions will be.

In some church circles, such honesty would be perceived as immaturity or as something to hide. But that's not the way Jeremiah writes, nor is it the way he lives his faith.

This is the beauty of what we see in Jeremiah's writing. This is gut-level realism. This is him demonstrating what it looks like to walk, with God, though moments that are not always pretty, but are always real. This is what a spiritual journey looks like. And I am thankful that Jeremiah gives us a look at his.

Blessings on you as you read.

Introduction

As I took my "Walk With God", I thought of how Good is the enemy of Great.

At this point in my life, I'm a teacher, spiritual leader and all-around "good" person. I've made it, right?

No, I haven't. I can't become comfortable with being good. It is the enemy of Great.

Several prominent men in the bible were Great but got comfortable with being good.

David was great. He slayed Goliath, became the king of Israel and wrote Psalms. But he set up a man to be killed, so he could hide a dalliance with his wife, which produced a child.

Solomon was the wisest man to ever live, but he had several wives and concubines.

Samson had immense power, but he was arrogant and had a weakness for women.

What do they have in common? They had the potential for greatness, but they were comfortable with being good.

I relate to them.

Through every chapter of my life, I've been comfortable with being good.

In high school, I had the potential to be the valedictorian. There was nothing stopping me. I was "gifted."

I cared more about sports than school, though. I was too busy watching Terrell Owens blow up, instead of blowing myself up.

Heading into college, I had the tools to be Great. I was a charismatic, smart kid with leadership potential.

Others noticed it.

My Communication's professor, Dr. Mark Goodman, said (in front of the class): "I respect Jeremiah, because he's a smart man."

Instead of being honored, I worried that my classmates would hate one me.

He was exalting me, but I wanted to be nondescript.

After college, I worked at my hometown newspaper. It was a terrific opportunity, but I didn't respect the position.

I didn't make the most of the opportunity. I arrived on time, not early and didn't honor my craft.

More chances presented themselves. I was the co-host of "Bully Barkline" and wrote for Genespage.com, a Scout.com affiliate. I didn't prepare for the show or put time into becoming a skilled writer.

When I moved to Texas, I worked security. I didn't take the job seriously. I felt that it was beneath me.

I moved from "The Sip" to "H-Town." Everything looked good on paper.

Being good hadn't yielded results. When I gave my life to Christ, he woke me up.

How did he do it?

One night, while I was in the middle of a work shift, I said that I wasn't going to do something. An older co-worker checked me: "You're a young man. It's embarrassing that you're behaving in such a manner."

After the encounter, I did some soul-searching. I got my act together. My work performance improved. A few months later, I was hired as a paraprofessional in Cy-Fair I.S.D.

Given an opportunity to cover the NCAA tournament in 2015, my mindset had changed.

It was a surreal experience. Grant Hill was there. National writers were there. Coach K was there. George Bush Sr. was there.

Sitting on press row, I didn't write or say anything. I was "star-struck."

A voice spoke to me: "Jeremiah, you said you want to be great. Then you need to study these great people."

I studied the sideline reporter, Tracy Wolfson, and how she prepared to interview a coach or player. I studied the other writers and asked questions. I studied Coach K and how he conducted himself, even when he chastised me for calling his players showboats(although they were showboating).

It carried over into other areas of my life. I studied, Ben, the teacher that I served under. He's assertive like I am. But he's more chill about it. He had a great rapport with the students, too.

Mirroring his traits, I developed a Great rapport with my Club Rewind kids.

In my spiritual life, I have several mentors. Great men of God. They've taught me to get up early, study the word, be a good steward, sacrifice for others, handle situations in a proper manner and to love on people.

I'm no longer comfortable with being Good, because it's the enemy of Great.

I leave you with two things.

1. Are you Great?

2. If you're not, what can you do to become great?

God Bless, Jeremiah

Part I

The Blueprint For Greatness

08/28/16

Sunday's Reflection: "I Am Great"

As I took my "Walk With God", I thought of my first circle-up with the kids.

I wanted to set a tone. So, to conclude it, I had the kids chant: "I'm Great!!!"

My first assignment was a "Your Purpose" graphic-organizer activity.

The kids wrote down "Their Why's" (Three most important people). My babies wrote them quickly…encouraging.

I explained the classroom rules, where the last rule was to "Be Great."

After explaining the rules, I broke down the 10 Rules for Greatness:

1. Be Gentlemen and Ladies
2. Always Say Thank You
3. Encourage Others
4. Remain Positive
5. Don't Worry About Affirmation
6. Put Others First
7. Always Do Your Best
8. Accept Responsibility
9. Honor Your Parents
10. Do What You're Supposed To Do

Then I discussed our Greatness Agreement (Social Contract).

And finished with the "Greatness Board" explanation.

Notice a theme. I wanted the word "Great" in their spirit. The word good can't be spoken. Not even by me.

While Monday was a great start, Tuesday was a little rough and frustrating. I wasn't prepared. I didn't perform to expectations.

When I got home, though, I looked at one of my student's, Caroline, "First-Day Film."

She wrote that she learned how to "Be Great" on her first day…wow.

Wednesday, I was encouraged that three of my kids wanted to become writers.

One of them, Mya, wrote me a beautiful story: "Mr. Short Saves The Day."

I've framed it already. (Still got it)

Thursday, I distributed classroom roles, which were based around what my kids want to be when they grow up.

I have a Classroom Narrator and Author. Their job is to chronicle the day.

My student, Robert, who wants to rap, is the Classroom "Hype Man."

Friday, everything slowed down.

Once my kids completed their "Your Purpose" activity, I shared my story.

I told them that I was GT (Gifted,Talented). But I played around in school and didn't accomplish what I should have, because I didn't believe in myself.

That changed, though, when I realized that I was great. I got my act together and now stand before them.

I told them: "Never let anyone tell you that you're not great."

The words resonated with them. They even checked me for saying good instead of great three times. My punishment was to have lunch with them.

Before I left, I looked at my student's, Jeffrey, "Your Purpose" activity.

Under the "Why I'm Awesome" portion, he wrote: "I Am Great."

I leave you with two things.

1. What's Your Purpose?
2. Are you speaking life or death into those in your sphere of influence?

God Bless, Jeremiah

09/04/16

Sunday's Reflection: "Live The Great Commission"

As I took my "Walk With God", I thought about how we don't need to earn a commission but live the Great commission.

Monday, I wasn't adequately prepared to teach. I push through, but I feel that I was too tough on my kids.

Tuesday, I apologized. As a result, the day went smoother.

Wednesday, I realized why I entered the profession. After playing a motivational message from "Inky Johnson", I asked the kids what it made them think about. I was encouraged that seven or eight kids had responses. It set a positive tone for the day.

The kids were participating and engaged. During Math, I jumped up and down as my kids raced to answer the problems.

When I gave them a "brain break", one of my kids, Michelle, shut it down "And1" style. She did a handspring. Watch out Simone Biles.

After the brain break, the kids calmed down and concentrated for Science. The kids gathered around me for the experiment--making their predictions. I was pumped. Great day!!!

I'd love to say that Thursday and Friday were great days like Wednesday. They were not. Both days were up and down. I did learn, though, that I shouldn't overreact to simple misbehavior.

Why do I say that? I was frustrated that my kids weren't on-task during math. I wanted perfection. As I reviewed my kid's math quiz, I saw that they'd retained the information.

I must relax and allow the educational process to happen. It's tough for me to do. I approach every day trying to make up for the ten years that I wasn't living up to my potential.

The lesson I learned was a Christian one. As Christians, we want to force the issue. We want to show God that we're his number-one "Fan."

We want to show him that we love him more than the other Christians

We want to bring people to Christ and earn our commission from God. But that's not following God's commandment. He wants us to "connect" people to him, not connect them to ourselves or our church.

People aren't baptized in the name of "Jeremiah."

They're baptized in the name of the Father, Son and Holy Spirit.

Last week's "Night of Worship" at Houston Northwest Baptist Church was the true embodiment of the Great Commission.

Steve Bezner (Houston Northwest's pastor), Blake Wilson (Crossover Bible Fellowship's pastor) and Adrián Amézquita (Houston Northwest's Spanish pastor), stood side by side.

Race didn't matter. Denomination didn't matter. Culture didn't matter. God mattered.

They didn't care about how the "Word of God" was heard. They cared that it was heard.

My student gave me the perfect note on Monday. It read: "In God We Trust."

She's right. We need to.

Don't Earn A Commission, Live The Great Commission.

I leave you with two things.

1. Are you trying to earn commission or live out the "Great Commission"?

2. If you're trying to earn commission, how could you start living it out?

God Bless, Jeremiah

09/11/16

Sunday's Reflection: "Everything Comes In Its Time"

As I took my "Walk With God", I thought of a statement from one of my kids, Serena.

Before school, the other kids were complaining that the breakfast hadn't arrived yet. Seemingly annoyed by the complaining, she stated(serenely): "Everything comes in its time."

Sage wisdom from a nine-year-old. But she is so right. Everything does come in its time.

I had a conversation with some co-workers the same day about success.

When is it supposed to happen?

Why does it happen?

Your role?

The vessel?

Our purpose?

Questions we ask ourselves. Christians and Non-Christian.

But should we question God's timing for our life?

As one of my kids, Jeffrey, put it, who doesn't trust God?

He knows when things are meant to happen.

I'll use my own life as an example.

Greatness was prophesied at an early age. I wanted to be successful. But I didn't know what it took. I relied on my talent and rested on my laurels.

God had to put me through some trials. College struggles. Financial struggles. Professional struggles. Personal struggles. Spiritual struggles.

Those struggles prepared me for where I am now.

Drawing from my experiences and mistakes, I can tell those 22,23 and 24-year-old's not to get caught up on comparing themselves to their peers.

If they do, they'll get depressed. They will have friends who are more successful personally, professionally and spiritually.

They may want what others have. But God knows they're ready for it.

Quick Personal Example: My first payroll check as teacher got sent to the wrong bank account. It was "bank error."

I got the situation rectified (apparently, that's an A.C.T. word). I never stressed, though. I have money saved.

It's in stark contrast to the 23-year old Jeremiah who bought clothes that he didn't need with his first check as an adult and purchased frivolous things with his student-refund checks.

The point: 23-year-old Jeremiah wanted to spend money. 31-year-old Jeremiah wants to save money.

That 23-year-old wasn't ready for what God had for him. The 31-year-old is.

Last week, Malinda, my brother-in-law's mother, said: "That stuff in you had to come out."

It did have to come out. But when God wanted it to.

Everything Comes In Its Time.

I leave you with two things.

1. Are you trusting God's timing?

2. If you're not, start trusting it. God has a plan for your life. Allow him to execute it.

God Bless, Jeremiah

09/18/16

Sunday's Reflection: "The Blueprint"

As I took my "Walk With God", I thought about family.

Two years ago, my Aunt Florence, who was a second mother to me, passed away. Her death impacted the entire family.

Listening to the stories at her funeral, others were impacted by her loss, as well. I can only hope to affect lives the way she did.

I feel that I'm starting to.

On Friday, a parent affirmed me, saying: "Your heart is in the right place, keep doing what you're doing and you're going to go a long way."

I was honored.

For years, I didn't know if I'd make an impact. In many conversations, I stated that I didn't have "The Blueprint" for success.

But it was in front of me the whole time. My family was The Blueprint.

The Smith's (Dad's Family)

They're a cohesive family. They'll find a reason to have a get together.

Uncle James is coming home from Atlanta for the third time this month. Let's have a barbecue.

"Crow" is cool like that.

He's devoted to family. If something is going on with a family member, he's driving from Atlanta to Macon to support or handle the matter.

He calls my grandma, Eva Kate, every day.

His sister, Linda, is an encouragement to me. She's experienced traumatic events, but she's never acted like a victim.

When I visited my dad for the summers, I stayed over her house. She taught me to respect my parents and elders, even if they've wronged me.

That's why I love her.

Her father, Robert Hopkins, is gracious in speech. From the stories I've heard, he wasn't always that person.

But through his example, I know that people can change and become a new creation.

My grandma, Eva Kate, is a true matriarch. She's the real life "Madea."

As a child, I'd sit for hours and listen to her stories. Through those stories, I've learned many life principles.

Don't keep up mess. Don't tease people. Help People. Don't take MESS from anybody. Be Bold.

Her son--my dad--showed me how to be a man.

After he dropped out of school to help my grandma, he's never been unemployed. At times, he has worked two jobs. He didn't curse in front of me growing up or lose his temper.

He's very punctual. Even through my work struggles, I was always early to work, because he modeled it.

I knew he was proud of me. He was at every key event. He was "suited and booted", too.

When you tell him information, he's ambivalent, so you don't think her cares. Then I talk to family members, and he's brought it up to them in a glowing manner.

Ex: I told my dad that I was covering the NCAA Tournament. Apparently, he was going around bragging about it. And I thought he didn't care.

The McGowan's (Mom's Family)

Growing up, they were tough on me. I harped on it.

This summer, a co-worker challenged me to say three positive things about my mom's side of the family.

It shouldn't have been hard.

They are tough.

Family Gathering are basically what happens when you get a bunch of "Type-A" personalities in the same room. You better learn to speak up or they'll still your solo.

As kids, we would place bets on which one of our parents would get into an argument first.

But you know what everyone is…a leader.

Every person on my mom side--the kids and parents--are business owners, supervisors and teachers.

My mom's sister, Allean, is a business owner and supervisor. She may not know it. But I learned about giving from her.

Once, she said: "I don't loan money. I'll give it, but I won't loan it."

It's biblical. The borrower is the slave to the lender.

My mom's other sister, Sandra, has been my guardian angel.

When I graduated from college, she let me stay at her place and have one of her cars. I can never repay her.

Before the start of the school year, she bought a treasure trove of goodies for my babies.

She's selfless…always putting others first.

Another thing about her: She was the Valedictorian of her high school class. My Aunt's smart like that. I had to brag on her a bit. Love you Aunt Sandra.

My mom's other sister, Twanda, and her husband, Roy have been there for me, too.

When I needed money in college, they were always willing to help. There was a 15-minute lecture attached to it. But they gave it anyway.

They've done more than give me money.

When I was a kid, someone attempted to sexually assault me. The first person I told was my Aunt Wanda. If I hadn't told her, I don't know how I would have turned out.

Over the years, Uncle Roy has given me advice. He didn't think this "hoodlum" who was "smarter than the average bear" was taking heed.

But I was. Two situations stick out to me.

1. When I was in college, he talked to me about making sure that my vehicle stayed washed.

Simple, right?

He told me that he had a 1970's car when he was young, but it was always clean. I was listening but didn't hear what he was trying to tell me.

I advise people to focus on the little things. Ten years ago, he was sharing the same principle. But I didn't grasp it.

2. When I was racially profiled and put in jail for a day-and-a-half, I was worried about what people would think.

Uncle Roy: "The only people that I should worry about is my family and friends."

He was right. The friends I've talked to have said that they couldn't believe it. One friend said that when someone told him what happen, he said that it must be another "Jeremiah."

Thanks Uncle Roy for having my back.

My mom's brother, John Moore Jr. or "Moorhead" had my back, too. He's always held me in high regard. He told a friend that I was like a "professor."

When I was in college, I had a conversation with him about politics. He told me that I should go into the arena.

My response: "Politicians lie. I don't want to be one of them."

Uncle John: "Be the one who tells the truth."

Thanks for speaking life Unc.

I learned a lot from my grandparents.

My grandad, Floyd McGowan, was a great man. That man would give you his last dollar.

My biological grandfather, John Moore Sr., died when I was young. Floyd was the only one I knew. He never viewed us as his step-grandkids, though.

For example, when I was in middle school, he told my cousin Cyrus and I that he didn't care that we weren't his blood grandkids.

I miss him.

If I wasn't playing around in college, he would have seen me graduate. All forever regret that I didn't get to share the moment with him.

My grandma, Eddie Mae, has always lent an ear for me to vent. She's sharp as a tac, too. We get our intelligence from her.

She stressed academics. That's why my mom and her siblings killed it in school.

They were some of the best students to come through "Noxubee County."

My grandma stressing academics is why my mom and her siblings were able to come from a two-bedroom house and sleeping on the same bed to make something of themselves.

One of those people is my mom, Jeanette.

We haven't always had the best relationship. I have some legitimate gripes. But I've started to "Think about what I was thinking about."

Yes, my mom didn't treat me the best.

But what else did she do? She raised four kids, for the most part, by herself. We had somewhere to stay. We had what we needed.

In school-system speak, we were "At-Risk" kids.

Darn those labels. Three of us graduated from college. We stayed out of trouble and are productive members of society. She did something right.

Thanks Mom and sorry for not being a better son.

With all the talk about family, it comes back to "Flo."

She left a true legacy. Her funeral was an event. So many people were there. I tell people that my Aunt Florence's funeral reminded me of the movie "Big Fish."

In the movie, this great storyteller's son goes on a mission to disprove his father's stories about his life. At the end of the movie, the son realizes that his dad was telling the truth. He made the stories more entertaining while re-telling them, though.

Anyone that knew my Aunt Florence would tell you how she engaged in "big talk."

Then you go to her funeral and all the people she said that she knew were there. A state senator spoke at her funeral. Flo made "moves."

I want to leave the same type of legacy. I want people to know that I was here.

My family gave me the principles to do it.

Devotion (Uncle James).

Giving (Aunt Allean and Wanda).

Selflessness (Aunt Sandra).

Speaking Life (Uncle John).

Diligence (Dad).

Focus on the little things (Uncle Roy).

Sacrifice(Mom).

Boldness (Eva Kate).

Be gracious in speech (Robert Hopkins).

Cover offenses (Aunt Linda).

Wisdom (Eddie Mae).

Leave a legacy (Aunt Florence)

In Proverbs 22:6, Solomon writes: "Train up a child in the way he should go; even when he is old he will not depart from it."

I haven't departed from what my family taught me.

They gave me "The Blueprint."

I leave you with two things.

1. Find a way to honor your family today.

2. Think about your legacy and if you're leaving the right one.

God Bless, Jeremiah

Part II
Your Mindset Shapes You

09/25/16

Sunday's Reflection: "Fill Up Your Tank(Spirit)"

As I took my "Walk With God", I thought about oil tanks.

Why?

Earlier this week, I was having car problems. The car wasn't running smoothly. I checked the oil level. It was very low.

With the craziness of a new role and school year, I got off my usual routine. Part of that routine was checking the oil every Saturday.

After buying some oil, I filled up the tank. The car ran smoother.

All I had to do was fill up the tank.

How many times, as Christians, are things out of whack because our tank(spirit) isn't filled?

All the time.

How can we keep our tank filled? There are three ways.

1. Understand the Holy Trinity: We worship God, serve Christ and filled by the Holy Spirit.

2. Get In The Word: After understanding that, we must get in the word. It's not about memorizing scriptures. It's about understanding them and taking that time with God.

When you take time with him, you need to talk to him. He'll talk back.

A closed mouth doesn't get fed.

3. Fellowship: Surround yourself with Christians who'll encourage you and keep you sharp.

"Iron does sharpen iron.

I haven't said anything about going to a church. That's purposeful.

I don't believe going to a physical church is where you grow close to God. It can. Your personal relationship with God is more important, though.

I'm not saying don't go to church. I attend a church and serve in it. But think about your reason for attending every Sunday.

Are you going to learn the word? Or are you going because it's a social norm?

I didn't grow closer to God until I took walks with him, studied his word and had daily conversations with him.

By spending time with God, I understood how deep the Bible is-- Old and New Testament.

After coming to Christ, the New Testament was an easy book to study. Paul wrote that. John wrote this. Jesus said this. It's straight-forward.

The Old Testament was always harder to understand. But it shouldn't be. It's rich with many lessons.

Take Daniel for example: Daniel was so committed to God that even when the King Darius passed a decree to not pray to any other God, he prayed three times a day.

As a result, he was thrown into the "Lions' Den."

King Darius said: *"Your God whom you constantly serve will Himself deliver you."*

Daniel survived the night. His tank was filled, and God rewarded him for it.

Samson wasn't as committed.

Before his berth, an angel told Samson's mother in Judges 13:3-5 that his hair can't be cut.

His arrogance and lust got him trouble, though. He repeatedly disobeyed God and then married a Philistine woman, Delilah, although he was supposed to be delivering his people from her people.

She betrayed him. His hair was cut, and eyes were gauged out. God didn't abandon him, though. His hair grew back, and he regained his strength. He killed thousands of Philistines.

Samson was strong and accomplished much. But he couldn't fulfill the prophecy to deliver his people, because his tank wasn't filled.

When you get in the word, you'll become more transparent, accountable and reflective.

Fill Up Your Tank.

I leave you with three things.

1. Is your tank filled?
2. If not, how can you fill it?
3. Are you surrounding yourself with people who help you fill it?

God Bless, Jeremiah

10/02/16

Sunday's Reflection: "God's Got My Back"

As I took my "Walk With God", I thought about how God's got my back.

In my Sunday Reflection: "Fill Up Your Tank", I said that I had another issue with my car.

After I ate dinner at Christina, my sister, home, my car battery died.

Why is that important?

Last week, my cousin, Walter, was in town for work and my mother prepared a meal, so we could spend time with him.

If he wouldn't have come into town, then my battery dies in the morning, not that night. I would have been late to school and missed time with my kids.

God had my back like he does in every situation.

I'm still in the developmental part of teaching. It's tough. I must lesson plan, turn in paperwork and learn important data while managing a classroom. It can be overwhelming.

I have personal and spiritual struggles, too. Last weekend, I was going through some.

God intervened again.

Walter's stay in Houston was extended, and we had lunch after church. It was a needed distraction.

After lunch, Christina invited me over to watch football. I had to lesson plan. But I came over afterward.

The quality time with family got me in the right space. It set the tone for a great week.

During my first "Parent-Teacher" conference, I found out that one of my kids studied an extra hour for the "Reading Checkpoint", because she wanted to be a Lion, not a Gazelle. I need 18 of them.

I received a blessing that night. A friend, Robert Udoh, told me to "Stay The Course."

I needed that word.

The next day, I was introduced to the new "Math Coach."

Math is my "grow" area. I was excited meet someone who's considered one of the best at teaching it. I've already set up my first coaching session.

My classroom started to flow, as well.

The week ended on a tremendous note. I wrote a story with the kids--instructing them on how to structure an essay and add details.

Also, the classroom champion, Michelle, met her match. A rematch is in order.

A voice came to me the next morning: "Jeremiah, it's time."

An incredible calm came over me.

God's got my back.

I leave you with two things.

1.What is God trying to show you?
2. Allow him to reveal it.

God Bless, Jeremiah

10/09/16

Sunday's Reflection: "Replace That "I" With God"

As I took my "Walk With God", I thought about being humble.

On Monday, my school's new "Math Coach" modeled a lesson. I was in awe. I was in the presence of greatness.

In the presence of greatness, what do I do? I take notes.

To recap the lesson, the Math Coach asked me what I observed. I pointed out several things that I noticed and liked.

She said it was good that I was reflective enough to seek her out for help.

It's not hard for me to do, though. I want to be great teacher. The only way I'll become one is by studying a teacher who is already great.

The next day, I raised my energy level and incorporated some of techniques she taught me in other subjects, as well.

With the tips that I learned, I was able to implement the I(Do)/We (Do)/You(Do) "gradual-release" model with fidelity (We love that word at Thompson.).

Friday, I played a motivational message from Eric Thomas, my kids yelled: "What Up, What Up, What Up…It's your boy ET."

I knew the day was going to be great. And it was.

We had a writing prompt where the kids had to answer a question: What's an important lesson that you've learned at school?

One of my students wrote: "Do the right thing, even when no one is looking."

I loved it.

One of my rules for greatness is to not expect affirmation. I believe in positive reinforcement, but I don't want to set my kids up for failure.

We ended the day with another great dance off. They're becoming more spirited and competitive.

I gave my kids a little surprise(popcorn). They were appreciative. The kids left the classroom with a smile on their face.

If there's anything I learned this week, it's that kids will always appreciate you more if you put them first.

That's not always the case in education. Some teachers are more concerned with being liked or receiving praise from administration. They'll put themselves before the kids in every scenario.

It's sad but true.

With Christianity, you can substitute kids with God. Too many Christians put themselves before God.

I expect selfishness in the World. We live in a selfish, me-first generation. Everybody wants to be a celebrity. Everybody thinks that they're "sweet."

People in the church shouldn't think they're sweet. But too many do.

In my church's children's ministry, we've been going through the story of Jesus.

The over-arching takeaway: He was humble.

When he was a boy, he sat among the elders and asked them questions.

Think about that for a minute. Jesus, one-third of the Holy Trinity, was trying to learn from others.

If Jesus can be humble, why can't we?

It's amazing what could happen if you take "I" from situations.

I don't agree. I am the way. I know what's best.

"Modern Christians" are turning people away from Christ because of their "I" mentality.

They think that they don't mess up. They think that they're perfect. They think that others aren't.

In Matthew 23:12, he writes: *"Whoever exalts himself will be humbled, and whoever humbles himself will be exalted."*

It's a scripture that forces you to ask a real question: Why would God exalt you if you're putting yourself before him?

I have no choice but to put God first. He's delivered me from so much.

Example: Three years ago, I was asked to come home and take care of someone. There's nothing wrong with taking care of someone. I had things I was trying to accomplish. I knew that I had it in me to accomplish them. But it was determined that I was only good enough to be a "caretaker."

The GT kid with a 130-plus I.Q. was only good enough to take care of someone. That's humbling. Darn near deflating.

God determined that I was good enough, though, and now I'm impacting lives.

How can I not put him first?

God doesn't need us, but he chose us.

Stop thinking that you're sweet and replace that "I" with God.

I leave you with two things.

1. Are you humbling yourself before the Lord?
2. If not, what is preventing you from doing so?

God Bless, Jeremiah

10/16/16

Sunday's Reflection: "You Get Back What You Put In"

As I took my "Walk With God", I thought about how you get back what you put in.

Last week, I purchased popcorn for my kids. I didn't mention that it was part of a fundraiser for another grade level.

I was happy to help my co-workers and their students.

What I didn't expect, though, was for one of them to ask if I needed "Dry-Erase" boards. It seems simple. But I was planning on buying some for my kids that weekend. A quick confirmation that I was doing the right thing.

Ain't God Good.

Tuesday, something interesting happened.

One of my kids, Maya, asked: "Why didn't you give me a high-five for getting the right answer?"

Another student, Darren, responded: "Don't expect affirmation."

They're paying attention. Don't expect affirmation is one of my rules for greatness.

The next day, for our writing assignment, I had the kids write five paragraphs on ET's "You Owe You" message.

They were asked to write the key points, identify the excuses they make, detail the traits of winners and losers and describe how they could become a winner.

One of my babies wrote that she needed to give 120, not 50. She also wrote that she wanted to be a lion, not a gazelle. She puts her words into action. For the most of the past two weeks, she's been a "Daily Lion."

Thursday, I utilized the dry-erase paddles for the "Science Checkpoint Review."

Friday, it payed dividends. The class improved on their first checkpoint scores by 13 percent.

In addition to the improved scores, I was thrilled to invite a few of my kids to the "Creative Writing Club."

They were excited.

I'm excited, too. I can't wait to make them great writers.

Another terrific Friday.

This week, my small investment paid off. If you invest in and show kids love, they'll show it back.

I get life from them.

I thank God every day for the opportunity to pour into my babies. I had a moment this week where I paused and thought: "I'm teaching right now. I can't believe it."

It's the story of my current life. I receive messages from people-- friends and family--thanking me for encouraging and inspiring them…inspires me.

It was surreal for someone to tell me: "God is speaking to me through you."

I have my faults and struggles. But God chose me as a vessel. My weaknesses and failures are helping others grow.

You Get Back What You Put In.

I leave you with two things.

1. How much are you investing in your relationships--personal, professional and spiritual?

2. Are you investing enough?

God Bless, Jeremiah

10/23/16

Sunday's Reflection: "Should I Sing A New Song?"

As I took my "Walk With God", I thought about if I should sing a new song.

A little over two years ago, I was eating a meal with some church group members. One of them said that a high percentage of the kids she taught were Black and Hispanic.

After a short diatribe, she said that most of them would probably never do anything.

Record skip moment, right?

Sadly, the other members nodded in approval. I was speechless.

Lately, the statement has been playing in my mind.

Teaching in Spring I.S.D., where most of the students are Black and Hispanic, she was talking about the kids that I shepherd.

I'm starting to ask myself: How can I attend a church where that's part of their culture?

My church is doing a "Life Together" series. With the political and social climate in America, it's a timely one to do.

I was troubled, though, when one of the pastors preached a sermon on unity.

There's nothing wrong with advocating for unity. But this pastor made excuses and allowances for the person who said that Black and Hispanic kids weren't ever going to be anything.

How could he preach about unity? In a wordy e-mail, I articulated those sentiments.

His response: "Thanks for the feedback."

I wasn't happy with the canned response and told him so. But after receiving some wise counsel, I realized that I was making it about myself, not God.

I always want to put God first. He's done so much in my life. He speaks to me in so many ways.

The most recent was while watching "Birth of a Nation."

The movie is based on the true story of Nat Turner's short-lived slave revolt in 1831. It's not historically accurate. But I understand what Nate Parker, the director and star of the movie, was trying to portray.

Parker was juxtaposing slavery with modern-day America. It's sad that not much has changed.

Turner, a pastor, was used by his master to calm slaves on other plantations for profit.

Eventually, he was convicted.

While delivering a sermon, he asks the slaves to sing a new, more powerful song. He empowers them and sets in motion a plan to rebel.

I don't want to hurt anyone, but I'm starting to wonder: Should I sing a new song(message)?

I love my church. There are some great mentors, and I take pleasure in serving in the Children's Ministry. But there are major cultural problems.

I vividly remember walking into church one Sunday with my badge on and a church member asked me if I was an usher (I'm a teacher in the Children's Ministry.).

Nothing wrong with being an usher, but why was that his first thought?

That's one example. But there are others.

My church is big on mission work, which is awesome. I'm troubled, though, that we have missionaries who regularly go to Kenya but walk past church members of the same descent and don't speak to or get to know them.

Don't read this reflection and think that I'm playing the victim. I'm not. I live for God, not people. People are in the church, though. They play a part in leading others toward Christ. They need to act like it.

How?

I'll state it plainly: If you want to grow spiritually, engender unity and have "Life Together", show it.

Actions speaks louder than words.

Are you willing to end a friendship for unity?

One of my babies, Michelle, did.

She wrote that she ended a friendship in second grade, because the other girls were bullies. It was a wise decision--as the kids got into trouble a few days later.

Makes you think. A seven-year-old has the character to end a friendship because it's the right thing to do.

But Christians won't do the same.

Should I sing a new song? Maybe not.

But I'm darn sure about to change my tune.

I leave you with two things.

1. Do you want unity in the body?
2. What can you do to prove it?

God Bless, Jeremiah

10/30/16

Sunday's Reflection: "Don't Play The Victim"

As I took my "Walk With God", I thought about the victim mentality that permeates our culture.

This week, I learned what happens when you don't play the victim.

Monday, the day started off great. I covered the four types of sentences: command, exclamation, statement and question. I jazzed-up my instruction by using my "art-dealer" voice.

The kids loved it.

While I was recapping the first chapter of "Bridge to Terabithia", one of my kids said that she heard a "command" sentence in the chapter. It was one of my prouder moments as a teacher.

My Writing and Reading instruction was on point. But my Math instruction wasn't. I introduced "Interpreting the Remainder" to the kids. They didn't understand the concept and weren't engaged.

I had to do something different. Instead of blaming the kids (playing the victim), I took the advice of an administrator and looked up online videos of teachers explaining "Interpreting the Remainder."

Tuesday, I re-introduced the concept with the tips I learned from the videos.

The kids comprehended the concept and were engaged in the learning process. They were so into the lesson that they didn't notice the Math Coach entering the room.

The next day, Bring-A-Parent-To-School Day, I played the kids "Leaders Go First" by Inky Johnson. I asked them to write three paragraphs on the topic. Most of the kids had great responses.

One student said that she could only come up with one sentence. I told her that one sentence could have an impact. And it did.

She wrote that it's important to lead, because you can inspire others…mic drop.

Later on that day, the kids participated in an activity where they had to represent every step of Interpreting the Remainder. Not only did they represent every step, they demonstrated mastery of it.

Friday, I concluded the week by working through interpreting the remainder word problems with the kids. It was so fun. The kids were captivated, engrossed and gaining additional practice.

This week, if I had blamed the kids for not understanding a concept, then that wouldn't have had my best week instructionally.

Thursday morning, my Uber driver said that she "liked my perspective."

I was referred to as "damaged" most of my life when I played the victim. Now, people love my perspective.

I can only thank God's saving grace for delivering me.

Don't Play The Victim.

I leave you with two things.

1. Do you play the victim?
2. If you stopped playing the victim, how much better would your life be?

God Bless, Jeremiah

11/06/16

Sunday's Reflection: "It's All How You Look At It"

As I took my "Walk With God, I thought about how it's all how you look at it.

Last Friday, before school ended, I found out that some kids stole their classmate's shoe. We couldn't find the shoe.

Following dismissal, I searched for the shoe with one of my students who was shadowing me until her mother arrived for the parent-teacher conference. I found the shoe in my closet.

I didn't care that I found the shoe. I cared about who stole the shoe and what consequences to give.

Then my student opined: "At least we found the shoe."

I paused and thanked her for saying it. Her statement reminded me of something my baby cousin, Reggie, said ten years ago.

I had a conversation with him on a variety of topics. After I told him my perspective on something, he opined: "Well…That's one way of looking at it."

It tripped me out. He was nine-years-old and spewing gems.

I told my Aunt Twanda, his mother, what he said.

She responded: "Yea, he's very articulate."

Two similar statements--ten years apart--illustrating the same point. It's all how you look at it. It's a matter of perspective.

Two weeks ago, I wrote about my church and how I didn't know if they genuinely wanted unity.

After attending our fall festival and seeing the incredible mix of people enjoying "Life Together", I realized that I was looking at it wrong.

At the fall festival, I had a great conversation with a gentleman from a partner church, Crossover Bible Fellowship, about the C1/C2/C3 dynamic. We talked about how you must be open to everyone and willing to adapt.

People see things through different lenses. Socio-Economic. Cultural. Biblical.

Even with our different experiences, we must learn to adapt. I know that I'm learning to.

I'm persistent, diligent, direct and passionate. I'm aware, though, that not everyone looks at those traits that way.

Persistence can be looked at as forceful or too aggressive. Diligence (4 a.m. wake-ups) can be looked at as manic, workaholic behavior. Passion can be looked at as anger. Direct speech can be looked at as attacking speech.

I don't look at it that way. But someone else might.

It's All How You Look At It.

I leave you with two things.

1. Are you looking at people and situations through the proper lens?
2. If not, how could you start looking at it the right way?

God Bless, Jeremiah

Part III

Failing Don't Make You A Failure

11/13/16

Sunday's Reflection: "Failing Don't Make You A Failure"

As I took my "Walk With God", I thought about my first failing as a teacher.

Monday, my kids had their second Math Checkpoint. Looking at the scores, I saw that most of them failed.

If it wasn't for a staff meeting, I would have cried. I was in a funk. I prepared the kids adequately. At least that's what I thought.

Selfishly, I wondered: How can I explain these scores? How do I recover from this?

I caught myself, though. I was asking the wrong questions.

I should have been asking: What can I change? Why did the kids struggle with the test? How can I keep the kids motivated?

While reviewing the checkpoint with the kids, I answered the questions.

I noticed that the kids struggled with the word problems, not the concepts.

Thankfully, our wonderful Math Coach introduced a new "Problem-Solving" model, which will help the kids process word problems more efficiently.

Also, I realized that I was moving too fast while instructing and not clearing up misconceptions.

To keep the kids motivated, I told them that greatness is expected, but it won't come overnight. It'll take hard work.

Friday, my kids made me proud.

I was observed as part of a district walkthrough. The kids were well-behaved, engaged and active participants in the learning process.

Due to a successful walkthrough, the teachers were rewarded with a "free-jeans" week.

This week, I experienced a failing, but I knew that I wasn't a failure by the end of it.

I've come a long way. I didn't always possess such a growth mindset.

While I was blessed with talents and gifts, I failed at life--especially in the work arena.

As a struggling writer, I was the master of odd jobs. I was the master of getting let go from those odd jobs, too.

I worked at a "Cheese Plant" in college. I was let go.

I worked in the kitchen at a nursing home in college. I was let go.

I worked at a "Chicken Plant" after college. I was let go.

I worked at a farm and convenience store. I was let go from both.

I was the definition of a person who "couldn't hold a job."

I started to think I was a failure. There was a point where I wondered if I should be here on this earth. I should have never thought that way.

Instead of feeling sorry for myself, I should have asked: Why am I failing?

The answer: I didn't require excellence from myself.

Example: During my senior year of high school, my mom got on me about my grades.

I deadpanned: "I just want to pass."

The crazy part is that I almost didn't. I was three months behind on my "Senior-Exit" Project, because I didn't want to edit a rough draft.

I hated to write.

Ironic, huh?

I should have been the Valedictorian. But I wanted to "pass."

That's how weak my mentality was back then. I had the nerve to play the victim as an adult when I was ok with being mediocre.

We need to ask ourselves: Was that my best?

I get to work at 7 a.m. But could I get there at 6:30?

I made a B. But could I make an A?

I have good relationships with people. But could I have great relationships with people?

Sports is the easiest arena to measure if you're giving your best.

Nick Saban, Alabama's head coach, understands it more than anyone.

His teams can win a game 38-7, and he'll spaz out at the post-game press conference about the cheap, late touchdown his team gave up.

To some coaches, that's not a big deal. To Saban, it's the end of the world. He knows that a minor slip up will show up at some point.

That was my life. Those weak areas caused me to fail as an adult.

My grudge-holding ways caused me to fail in relationships with my siblings--Roberto and Christina.

Berto and I were tight during our adolescence. I looked up to him. How could I not? He was cool, popular and a track star.

After he headed off to the military, though, our relationship eroded. We fought--figuratively and literally. It got to point where we would agree to disagree.

That lasted for over ten years.

One night that changed. My best friend, Demetris, checked me: "You're just jealous of him."

He was right. I wanted to be more than his smart ★★★ little brother.

I called Berto and apologized for being jealous of him.

Friday, my kids wrote to him for "Veterans Day."

Look at God.

I was tight with my sister, Christina, growing up, as well. Even when she was the cool college student, we talked on the phone about life.

Our relationship started to suffer, though, while I was in college. It got so toxic into adulthood that I didn't even attend her vow-renewal service.

That's how much hate I had in my heart.

After I came to Christ, though, I started to think about…what I was thinking about.

My sister pretty much raised me, allowed me to stay with her when I moved to Houston and laid the blueprint for a successful post-college life.

Over the past two years, our relationship has been restored. I attend a life group at her home on Friday's. We're growing in Christ together now.

Ain't God Great.

He's brought me through so much. He's renewed my mind, body and spirit.

He can do it for you, too.

You may feel that you've failed in life and think that God can't use you. But you're wrong.

You may have an addiction. Alcohol. Gambling. Porn. Sex. You may have done another person wrong or committed a heinous crime.

None of that matters. Moses was a murderer. David slept with another man's wife. Paul was a Pharisee and persecuted followers of Christ.

God used them. He can use you, too.

Let him turn your "mess" into a message.

"What Makes The Great Great" has a profound line: There is no failure, only feedback. Live and learn.

Failing Don't Make You A Failure.

I leave you with two things.

1. Do you feel like you're failing at life?
2. Give it to God. You're not a failure in his eyes.

God Bless, Jeremiah

11/20/16

Sunday's Reflection: "Plant A Seed"

As I took my "Walk With God", I thought about planting a seed.

Monday, I attended a new-hire training event. The speaker, Robert Jackson, shared the story of a former student.

After many years, he saw the student in the mall with his family. The student approached him and thanked him for everything that he did for him.

Not the most abnormal interaction. But the student was a "problem-child" when he taught him.

Following that story, he said that we must "plant seeds." We may not see them grow for 18 years. But we must plant them anyway.

I marinated on his message all week, which was a tough one. The teachers had to prepare the kids for three checkpoints.

My kids did progressively better on each checkpoint. Friday's (Science) was the most encouraging, though.

The scores weren't to my expectations. But there were some positives.

Before the checkpoint, I polled my kids. I asked how many studied the extra material that I e-mailed to their parents. Five kids raised their hands.

After running the scantrons, I saw that all of them passed, except for one. And that kid barely failed.

Two of them stick out.

The first kid, Robert, is one of my "Huck Finn's."

It's a constant battle to keep his behavior together. Something sparked him, though. He told me that his mom didn't even make him look at the material. He did it on his own. He raised his score by 29 points.

The second kid, Arianna, had a rough week. She missed two days of school because of a family issue. Worried, I solicited the "prayer-warriors."

She returned to school Thursday. I talked with her at lunch about the situation. Her grandmother was held up that day on another part of town. So, she had to stay after school.

Everything happens for a reason. I was afforded a chance to review the material with her. After her grandmother picked her up, she studied the material for two hours.

She scored advanced.

When I told her the score, she screamed…too cool.

When the kids came in from recess, I talked to them about the checkpoint. I asked all the kids who studied the extra material to stand up. I let the class know that all of them did well.

I used it as a "teachable" moment. I talked to them about Greatness and what it takes to reach it. I told them that I'm tired of all that complaining about homework stuff.

I reiterated that I was the "GT" kid who was lazy and didn't work hard, because I was stuck on that my-mama-don't-love-me foolishness.

And that the things that I'm doing now…I should have been doing at 21. I have nobody but myself to blame. I'll do my part as a teacher. But they have to do their part, too. You can lead a horse to water, but you can't make it drink.

You could have heard a pen drop in the room.

Considering that it was a three-checkpoint week, I let the kids "Ju Ju That Beat" a few times. I did it again before dismissal…too hype in Mr. Short's room.

I planted the seed of greatness. It grew faster than I thought it would.

It's the natural flow of life. Once a plant grows, it sprouts seeds, and they grow, too.

Plant a seed.

It might grow into something that'll change the world.

I leave you with two things.

1. Are you planting seeds?
2. Are they the "right" ones?

God Bless, Jeremiah

11/27/16

Sunday's Reflection: "Be Like Oseola McCarty"

As I took my "Walk With God", I thought about Oseola McCarty.

Last Sunday, while flying to Mississippi, I finished up "What Makes The Great Great" by Dennis P. Kimbro.

In Chapter 9, he shared the story of Oseola McCarty, a washerwoman who never married or had kids.

She led a boring life. Her daily routine was, well, routine.

McCarty's daily routine: *She rose with the sun, drew water from a hydrant, and lit a fire under a huge black pot to boil white cotton garments, then scrubbed each item by hand before draping them across one hundred feet of line to dry.*

To end the day, she would rinse delicates and then meticulously iron every piece.

She did it diligently for years, even when her neighbors criticized her for "washing them white folk's dirty drawers."

Mrs.McCarty would die and no one would know her name, right? Wrong.

When Mrs.McCarty retired, she received a call from the bank? They wanted to know what to do with her savings.

She told them to give 10 percent to her church, split 30 percent of it between three relatives and donate the rest to the University.

The banker questioned: The University?

She responded: "Yes, the school here in town--Southern Mississippi. I want the money to go to some child who needs it. I'm too old to get an education, but now they can."

Her act was noble. But I'm sure you're thinking that her savings amounted to a few thousand dollars.

Wrong again.

Mrs.McCarty had amassed a small fortune (250,000 dollars).

How did she do it? Initially, she saved nickels and dimes. Those turned into passbook savings. Those turned into Christmas Club accounts to savings bonds to certificates of deposit to money market accounts.

The Oseola McCarty Scholarship Fund was established. The national media got wind of her story. People across the country were touched by it and matched her donation.

Her donation was the largest such donation to a Mississippi university by an African-American at the time.

Even with newfound fame, Mrs.McCarty remained humble.

McCarty's quote on her donation: "It's more blessed to give than to receive. When I leave this world, I can't carry nothing away from here. I live where I want to live. I couldn't drive a car if I had one. This is what I planned to do. Years ago, my race couldn't go to that college. But now they can."

She continued: "I can't do everything, but I can do something to help somebody. And what I can do I will do. The only thing that I regret is that I didn't have more to give."

Mrs.McCarty, this humble washerwoman, left a legacy.

Why? She did what she could.

You know what's sad, though? Most Christians don't get that all you have do is what you can.

They want to do too much. They want everyone to know how sweet or deep they are. And that just their political opinions.

It's sad but true. They're bold in letting you know how they feel about abortion, gay marriage, a wall or welfare (even if their grown kids are living with them rent free).

I'm not deriding people for having opinions. I'm a writer. I have plenty of them. I'm encouraging them to be bold in sharing their faith, too.

I had a great conversation with my Uber driver.

A little background: My driver was Filipino gentleman who'd converted to Christianity from the Muslim faith.

He asked me a challenging question.

Uber driver: "You know the difference between Muslims and Christians?"

Me: "What?"

Uber driver: "Muslims are willing to die for their faith."

Me: "Die…It's hard enough to get Christians to share it."

Sadly, my Uber was salient in his observation. Most Christians aren't willing to lay it on the line for their faith.

Most fall into what Craig Groeschel describes as "Christian Aetheism": Believing in God but living as if he doesn't exist.

They'll fool you, too. They'll share "Truth" or how many scriptures they know.

Lest they forget that "The Devil" tempted Jesus with "The Truth."

Are they trying to emulate him?

That bible--that contains "The Truth"--does tells us in 1 Corinthians 2:14 that "*the natural person does not accept the things of the Spirit of God, for they are folly to him, and he is not able to understand them because they are spiritually discerned.*"

Translation: Non-Christians aren't supposed to understand scripture. They don't have the spirit in them yet.

Why beat them over the head with it?

We need to show non-Christians our faith like Mrs. McCarty, not by sharing "Truth."

They need to see it in our lives. We can't be passive, gossip, engage in prejudicial behavior, show partiality, serve alcohol at Christian functions or share uninformed, strident political opinions.

If you're displaying these characteristics, why would someone want to know you or your God?

Mrs.McCarty understood who was number one in her life and was exalted for it.

Are you willing to mimic her?

Are you willing to "Do What You Can?"

Because it's enough.

Be Like Oseolo McCarty.

I leave you with two things.

1. Are you a Christian Atheist?
2. How can you show that God is in number one in your life?

God Bless, Jeremiah

12/03/16

Sunday's Reflection: "No Longer Running"

As I took my "Walk With God", I thought about my destiny.

Two weeks ago, I went home for Thanksgiving break. It was my fourth time returning home since moving to Houston and first extended stay since 2012.

I got to see some familiar faces. I got to be Jeremiah, be "Miah", be "Moot", be "J.Short", be myself.

Was I the same guy who my friends and family saw me as for years?

During the trip, I realized that maybe I'm something more now.

Example: While I was at home, I stayed with my grandma, Eva Kate. The last time I stayed with her in 2010 ended poorly. My grandma got up before me in the morning, and I had a "sorry" mentality.

Eventually, she had to put me out--due to my irresponsible behavior.

This time, I got up three hours before my grandma to get in the Word, to journal and read books. I was quite purposeful about showing her that I wasn't the same petulant grandson.

I shared a few of my Reflections with her. After I read "Failing Don't Make You A Failure", she teared up. My baby cousin, Pooh, messed with her about it.

She told me to keep up the "good work." Your Aunt said that you're going to be a preacher.

Tuesday, I visited a few people.

The first person I visited was Aunt Mae. I hadn't seen her in years.

Apparently, she talked to my grandma, Eddie Mae, about my visit and said that I was "dressed nice."

After visiting with my aunt, I chopped it up with Uncle John. I read him "The Blueprint."

To him, the Reflections were "tough" and "inspirational."

Later in that day, I stopped by the barbershop to chat with my childhood barber, James Miller. We usually talk about sports. But we talked about the importance of names and God. He wrote down a few pastors for me to check out.

I ended the day chilling with my best friend, Demetris. I had a chance to talk with his mother, Hattie Mae, too. I talked to her about where I was in life.

She wasn't surprised by my success, because I was never "troublesome", "smart" and had a "good attitude."

I appreciated her words. She doesn't know. But her advice through the years has helped me deal with several tough situations.

Thanksgiving Day, I spent time with family. Aunt Linda gave me the honor of praying over the meal. I was overwhelmed, but I held it together to say the prayer.

Saturday, my final day in Mississippi, was awesome, too. I visited my Aunt Lee and her daughter, Cassie. They're great women of God. I shared a few of my Reflections and talked about how to live a Christ-centered life with them.

We joked about how Aunt Lee's husband, Silas, always said that I'd be "smart."

On the way to airport, I had an interesting conversation with my step-brother, Curtis. He asked me if I was still into those (video)games.

I told him that I sold my game system and don't play them anymore.

That short exchange defined my trip and new walk. I'm not that same person. I'm something more.

When I returned home and reflected on the trip, I thought about the belief that people always had in me. I thought about my story and how it's helping people and might help more.

So, I came to the decision to turn my Reflections into books. I've already written one. One is in progress.

I know that I'm opening myself up--as there will be naysayers and people that will come against me. Heck, I had one person call my Reflections "Recreation" and others refer to them as "things."

There are people who refer to them as "powerful", "prophetic" and "inspirational", though.

I'm ready for the bad and good. That's the mission God has for my life. I'm taking it. He's protected me at every turn, even on the day that I was born.

My birth story is one that I've never shared publicly. After reading about Tim Tebow's birth story Saturday morning, the spirit led me to do so.

When I was 18, I found out that my mother closed her legs on my head as I was coming into the world. There's debate as to why. But it was confirmed by two elders on both sides of my family.

I could have died, but I didn't.

After learning the information, part of me thought that my mom treated me poorly growing up because she was ashamed of the mistake.

I darn sure never felt wanted. One situation always brings that thought home.

When I was in middle school, I entered the house with Demetris. My little brother chased us out the house with a knife. I told my mom when she got home, and she said that I must have "done something."

Maybe existing was doing something. My mom did tell me that she wishes that she had never met my dad at that "disco club."

Reflecting, God saved me at birth and from that childhood pain for a reason. I know now that I was meant to survive. I was meant to exist. I was meant to be Great.

God put me on an incredible journey.

I've gone from Moot (The Damaged Child) to Jeremiah (The Irresponsible Adult) to J.Short(The Controversial Columnist) to Mr. Short(The Teacher) to now--Jeremiah Short(The Author).

I'm no longer running from my destiny. It's mine, and I'm claiming it.

I leave you with two things.

1. What's your destiny?
2. How can you step into it?

God Bless, Jeremiah

12/10/16

Sunday's Reflection: "Blessed Be The Name Of The Lord"

As I took my "Walk With God", I thought about how his named is blessed.

Last Sunday, I wrote that I was "No Longer Running." God didn't waste any time seeing if I was telling the truth.

Later that night, I ran an errand and stopped at a fast-food establishment. I left my car "running." After receiving my order, I walked outside, and my car was gone.

Before spazzing out, I made sure that it wasn't a "Dude, Where's My Car?" moment. It wasn't. My car had been stolen.

I filed a police report and notified my apartment complex that I needed a key to get in my apartment.

While I was concerned about my vehicle, I had to get to work in the morning. I couldn't miss a day with my babies.

Thankfully, a church member volunteered to take me to work.

That moment made me understand the reasoning behind God putting kids in my life. They've become my "Why."

My Why got me to school at 6:30 a.m. after getting my car stolen at 6:30 p.m. the night before.

It was an important week, too. The teachers had to mentally prepare the kids for "Benchmarks."

My kids told me that they were nervous about them. I told them that I was nervous, too. But there's nothing to be nervous about. It's an opportunity to show how Great they are.

For my kids to understand greatness, though, they needed to know what it looked like. Dealing with an outside distraction, I had opportunity to model it.

So, that's what I did. I knew the mini-storm would pass.

It did.

Stuart Sheehan, who is the president of World Hope Ministries, is quite wise and a spiritual influencer.

I took advantage of that one-on one-time by asking a few questions.

1. How to be a responsible spiritual influencer?
2. How to balance family and spiritual responsibilities?
3. How to deal with being responsible for others?

Reflecting. if my vehicle hadn't been stolen, would I have been able to ask those questions?

Stuart wasn't the only person who supported me. Friends and family did, as well. I really appreciated it. I'm not much for affirmation. But it's good to know that someone has your back.

My mother let me borrow her vehicle Friday. One church member let me borrow their vehicle for next week. Another church member offered to let me borrow a vehicle until I sorted things out.

One of my "Students of the Week" said that I didn't have to get her a gift (I usually get the kids a small gift for receiving the honor.). She said that she knew that I had a tough week. I was touched.

Friday, during circle-up time, one of my students, Riley, said that she got up in the middle of the night to study her Social Studies notes. She passed the quiz…another "Lion."

Thursday, an administrator said that I had "grown."

I saw it Friday. While I reviewed for the Math benchmark, I instructed on a concept (Area Model). One of my kids, Serena, said that it was easier to understand than the last time.

She showed me the original notes. It was a jumbled mess. The current example was clearer and more understandable.

It's one thing to hear that you're growing. It's another to see that you are.

This week, God placed an obstacle in my path. Not only did I deal with it, I ran to it.

On Wednesday, a co-worker said that I was acting like nothing was wrong (although it was). She would be stressing.

She doesn't know what I know and what Job knew: *"The Lord gave, the Lord has taken away, blessed be the name of the Lord."*

I leave you with two things.

1. What obstacle do you have blocking your blessing?
2. How can you run to it?

God Bless, Jeremiah

12/17/16

Sunday's Reflection: "Greatness Was Upon Them"

As I took my "Walk With God", I thought about "Greatness."

Last week, I told my kids to not be nervous about their Benchmarks. Assessments weren't something to be apprehensive about but a chance to show how Great they were.

I didn't know if they'd answer the challenge.

Monday, I reviewed for the Math and Reading Benchmarks. The kids had a few weak areas that concerned me. I told them to study the extra material that I sent home.

Following the Math exam, I checked the scores. They didn't perform up to my expectations, but they improved from their last "Checkpoint."

I was encouraged. I let the kids know that they improved because of their studying. But if they studied more, they could take it to another level.

They took heed--scoring 12 percent above the rest of the district on their Reading Benchmark. I was pumped.

We had one more Benchmark…Writing.

For their Writing Benchmark, I challenged them to study more. I didn't mean one hour. I needed two, three, four or five.

The kids scored nine percent above the rest of the school district…beast mode.

To celebrate, "We Got Turnt Up."

Friday, I told the kids that they all were the "Students of the Week" for their Benchmark performance.

I left them with a caveat: They could do better.

Seven kids were one or two questions away from passing their Writing Benchmark. Those students need to get at least two questions better before we take the STAAR.

With a long week of testing, the kids got to relax a bit. We had a "Holiday Party" and battled another classroom in a dance off. The week and semester ended on a high note.

The stories behind the Benchmarks made the week even better.

Take the Math Benchmark.

Two of the kids that passed it failed the Math STAAR last year.

Michelle didn't just pass, though, she was advanced.

Monday, she said that she'd study like it was a "volleyball" game. I guess she did.

For the Reading Benchmark, I found out that 13 of 21 kids had studied. Their scores reflected it.

After the Writing Benchmark, I polled the kids on how many hours they studied. Only one raised their hand for one hour. More raised their hand for two hours. More raised their hand for three hours. More raised their hand for four hours. One student studied five hours…amazing.

I asked Maya what she was thinking about as she studied.

Maya: "I want to be a writer and know I have to get better"

Love that growth mindset.

A couple of weeks ago, Jennifer, who was my highest-performer, told me that she wasn't comfortable with her placement in my room. (She was moved from another room after the first nine weeks.).

Friday, she gave a touching speech …saying that she would miss her classmates. And then danced when I notified that Writing Benchmark score was the highest mark in the school.

At the school "Sing-A-Long", she was highlighted as the classroom representative in the Spelling Bee.

Stories like these are the reason I decided to take the path that I did.

This week, my kids realized that "Greatness Was Upon Them."

It's my job to make sure that they reach it.

I leave you with two things.

1. Do you believe that you're Great?
2. Know that you are.

God Bless, Jeremiah

Part IV

The Light Came On

01/01/17

Sunday's Reflection: "That Moment"

As I took my "Walk With God", I thought about "that moment."

After quitting my security job, I struggled financially. One month, I had trouble paying bills, and few churches helped me pay them.

Houston Northwest was one of those churches. I didn't know much about it. I needed help, though.

While I was standing in the "waiting" area of the administrative building, a voice told me: "This will be your home."

I listened and started attending HNW, even participating in a Revelation's bible study. It was a little intense, but I loved it. I joined a home group, dwell group and gave my life to Christ.

It was nice to be part of a community. My comfort zone was disturbed, though. I was uncomfortable going to church with so many white people.

I had a conversation with a friend about my dilemma. I told him that I had issues going to church with all these "white folks."

He responded: "Do you think they're good people?"

My response: "Yes."

He responded: "That's the only thing that's important."

During the first year, I healed from scars of the past and got my first job in education.

Things were looking up.

Around that time, I started to question God and fight him about attending the church.

Me: A girl said that my babies wouldn't amount to anything. You sure this is the place for me?

That started a year-long conversation with him.

God, I'm dealing with macroaggressions.

People don't like my approach. They're saying I'm too aggressive, critical and "radical."

God, these people didn't even ask me how I was doing when my aunt died. All one person had to say was "Sorry for missing the announcement."

God, I wasn't announcing the gender of a baby. My aunt died.

God, they want me to change, to be less intelligent, to be safe, to be less than great.

God, I can't do that. Flo told me to never "compromise" myself.

God, I like rap music. I want the people around me to understand the reference "I'm going to sip my tea on that."

I want to speak directly without someone making a big deal about it.

God, I need to go where I'm celebrated, not tolerated.

That dialogue continued until God answered.

As I took those walks with him, I realized that some of the issue were a result of culture shock. I had problems with part of the church but not the church.

The church had supported me, as well.

My church supported me when I was homeless. They supported me when I went on mission trips. They supported me when my vehicle was stolen.

I'll never forget those things.

When I started attending my church, I took a Foundations class, too. I was blessed to learn from Stuart Sheehan and Craig Kendrick. Not many people get that opportunity.

I've learned how to be a man of God from Allen Tate and Dobie Weise. I love them and appreciate their mentorship.

People have "grown" by knowing me.

My church helped an unfocused boy become a purposeful man.

Through the stewardship of Dr. Steve Bezner, I've witnessed a transformation of the congregation. He's the reason that I didn't leave the church.

He's attempting something ambitious, daunting and challenging. He's attempting to turn an ultra-conservative, predominantly white, cliquish church into a multi-cultural one.

That's bold.

According to an article, Pastor Steve is one of the "wokest" (most socially aware) white pastors in America...America.

I get to call that man pastor.

God, why did I ever question you?

I understand "that moment."

I leave you with two things.

1. Are you questioning God?
2. Has he answered you?

God Bless and Happy New Year, Jeremiah

01/08/17

Sunday's Reflection: "I Can't Fail"

As I took my "Walk With God", I thought about how I can't fail as a leader.

Recently, I finished "The Gold Standard" by Mike Krzyzewski or "Coach K", who I covered in 2015.

In the book, there's an excellent quote from Coach K: "When leaders make clear their willingness to change, it establishes an environment in which everyone can be comfortable adapting."

I took two things from it.

1. Leaders need to be fallible

2. If you're fallible, those you lead will be fallible and more amenable to change.

It hit home Friday.

For the kid's writing prompt, I chose a scary topic. I asked them to write about what it would feel like to be your teacher.

As I expected, it was enlightening.

One of my babies, a talented young writer, shared her story. She wrote that Mr.Short can be mad, happy and then at the same time want to give you a treat. She could articulate when I would get upset, at who and why. I was amazed and impressed. But it made me reflect.

Maybe I should be Happy Mr.Short more.

After my kids' Reading quiz, I realize that they were adapting to their leader. I talked to the kids about the quiz. Most of them made 100's.

A couple of kids shared that they looked up videos and extra material, even though I didn't tell them to.

They were taking ownership of their learning.

It was apropos that I played Eric Thomas' Lion and the Gazelle video to indoctrinate my new kids to the culture of the "Greatness" room that morning.

Following the video, I asked the kids what the difference between the lion and the gazelle was.

After a few responses, one of my kids, Serena, said: "The gazelle gets up because they have to…the lion gets up because they want to."

I responded: "Yes. That's it."

I talked to them about greatness. I told them: "Great leaders don't make more followers. …They make more leaders. I'm trying to make all of them leaders."

The 21 Irrefutable Laws of Leadership has a superb line: "If you think you are leading and turn around to see no one following, then you are just taking a walk."

These leaders are focused on their title, not the responsibility that comes with being a leader. They're not accountable and display an unwillingness to change. They never reach greatness and may lead others the wrong way.

I don't want to be that type of leader. I feel that pressure. I'm not allowed to mess up.

Wednesday night, I had a dream.

In the dream, two relatives died and another relative (Aunt Florence) who passed away was living.

The dream was vivid. God was telling me something. I interpreted those two dying relatives as the people who are depending on me for life.

I realized that Flo never got to physically finish out her legacy. But her spirit lives through me.

How could I not live for her? She thought I would be great.

When others in the family dogged me for years (telling me to give up that writing), she spoke life. She said that "breakthrough would come."

And it did.

I'm not mad at those who doubted me, though. Sight is for those who live in the present. Vision is for those who can see the unseen. They couldn't see what God had for me because he had it for me.

Not for them.

God is directing my steps.

I can't fail.

I leave you with two things.

1. Are you a great leader?
2. If not, how could you become one?

God Bless, Jeremiah

01/15/17

Sunday's Reflection: "Follow God's Lead"

As I took my "Walk With God", I thought about how I need to "follow God's lead."

Last week, I had a conversation with my boy, Reggie. We discussed a variety of topics. During the conversation, he brought up that I haven't done any sports writing in a while.

His comment caused me to reflect on that time as J.Short. I co-hosted a radio show (Bully Barkline), got to write about my alma mater (Mississippi State) and chronicled two mission trips with "Athletes In Action."

I'll never forget the two NCAA tournaments that I was blessed to cover. I asked Roy Williams a question, and he cried. It was on "Sportscenter."

When I covered the Elite Eight at NRG, I got checked by Coach K, the Coach K, for insinuating that his players were "showboats."

How cool is that?

After my first year in education, I received an invitation to the 2015 NSSA(National Sports Writers and Sportscasters Association) Hall of Fame Weekend.

While I was there, I was afforded the opportunity to pick Bob Ryan's, a famous sportswriter, brain.

I asked him how I could become a better writer and who should I study to become one?

He said to "read, read, read, read, read." That's literally how he put it.

Then he told me to study Mike Vaccaro, who has won Sportswriter of the Year countless times. He's the best in the business.

Due to those experiences, I'll forever have stories to tell.

There was an interesting question posed at my brother-in-law and sister's home group: Should we forget about God's will for our life or what we think God's will for our life is?

Sounds crazy. But it's a good question.

I thought God's will was for me to write. Teaching was supposed to be a short detour. God had something else in store.

Opening my heart to kids, God redirected me. I love pouring into my babies. And I understand now why God put me on this path.

Before I started teaching, I was an opinionated sportswriter but didn't write with heart. My kids give me one, because they have mine.

Last Sunday, my church had its "Vision Sunday."

Instead of talking about the church budget and the next series, Pastor Steve Bezner shared some statistics from a BBC podcast, which called Houston the "City of the Future."

Why was Houston the city of the future? Pastor Steve cited the under-21 demographics: 51 percent Latino, 19 percent black, 8 percent Asian and 22 percent Anglo.

Pastor Steve said that the church needs to go with the future or...

Then I thought: That's my classroom. I'm training the future of America.

I've made an early impact on those future leaders. My message of hard work and greatness is already getting through to them.

There's an excerpt from "You Win In The Locker Room First" by Jon Gordon and Mike Smith which made me realize that it was.

You know your message was accepted by the team when you hear it being talked about in the locker room, on the practice field, in the cafeteria, the training room and to the media room.

My kids are part of a classroom, not a football team. But culture is culture.

Some examples.

Wednesday, the kids were at lunch and trying to get confirmation that one kid was named a "Daily Lion."

Thursday, during a "Creative Writing Club" session, I had the kids write an expository: "Why is practice more important than the game?"

Michelle, a talented writer and annual Daily Lion, quoted ET, saying: "I want to go from Great to Phenomenal."

Another child ended her expository by saying that she'll leave us with two things…too cute.

The culture that I've created has started to turn into academic success for my kids. They're still not where I want them, but they've improved.

My kids believe that they can be something. One parent told me that their child wanted to be singer but now she wants to be a Veterinarian because of my influence.

The room's energy is palpable, and others have taken notice.

Friday, after my Alternative Certification Program observation, the coach said that he "enjoyed" watching me.

It's important to handle this early success the right way. I can't be arrogant and must remain humble.

I have no choice but to handle it correctly. And I'm not going to complain about what God wants. I'll be J.Short again.

But for now, I'm going to "follow God's lead."

I leave you with two things.

1. Are you following God's lead?
2. If not, how could you start following it?

God Bless, Jeremiah

01/22/17

Sunday's Reflection: "What's Your Gap(Barrier)?"

As I took my "Walk With God", I thought about how to close gaps.

In the educational arena, educators are always trying to close them.

1. Why is my classroom management average?

2. Why is my instruction a step behind?

3. Why can't I connect with my kids?

If you're going to become a great teacher, you must answer those questions.

Thankfully, I've answered questions one and three, although it wasn't immediate.

During my first year in education, I struggled with classroom management and connecting with my kids. I was the "mean" leader. And had some frustrating days.

After some self-assessment, I realized that I needed to take a firmer approach from day one. If you're firm from day one, then you can gradually ease up. I learned how to properly group kids, as well.

Once I started developing rapport with my kids, I started to connect with them, too.

While I've closed two gaps, I still need to close my instructional gap. At times, they seem more like gaping holes. There were days at the beginning of the year where I didn't know what I was doing.

I could teach writing but everything else was a wash. Through sound coaching, I've filled some of those gaps.

One example sticks out.

During the second nine weeks, several of my kids were failing Social Studies. I told an administrator that they needed to study more.

He asked: "Have you modeled studying?"

My response: "Modeled studying?"

Honestly, I thought kids should know how to study by the time they reach the 4th grade. I was wrong.

What did I do? I modeled studying.

Before a quiz, I asked every one of my kids how they learn best.

I told them: "If you're visual learners, watch videos. If you're an auditory learner, then have someone call the notes out to you. If you can study independently, then study by yourself.

What happened? Kids that were failing are now making 100's.

My babies know their learning styles, too. About two weeks ago, one of my kids said that she was a visual/auditory learner. ...and doesn't like when people move around...too cool.

Understanding my kids' learning styles helps me instruct them more effectively.

Example: Two weeks ago, I was instructing on number patterns. The concept wasn't clicking with one of my kids. I remembered that she was a visual learner. So, I circled parts of the pattern with color markers. It clicked instantly.

As I've closed those instructional gaps, my kids are taking it to another level. And with my kids taking it to another level, I've started to experience a few professional victories.

While experiencing those victories, my "true" gap showed up. I'm afraid of success. If I examined the "root" of it, I'm afraid of the jealousy that comes with it.

I'll explain using cause and effect.

1. Cause: Professor calls me a smart man in front of the class.

Effect: During a final presentation, group members attempt to cross me up.

2. Cause: My boss openly praised me at a new job. Co-worker who is friends with my boss's wife starts to give me a hard time and sabotage work orders.

Effect: I'm fired unexpectedly, and it takes six months to find solid work.

3. Cause: During my first year in education, I dared to dress well, let it become known that I was a voracious reader and think ambitiously.

Effect: A few co-workers banded together to get me in trouble and knock me down a peg. One flat out lied. They made the last two months of the school year h★★★.

Due to that last example, I have a deep mistrust of white women in the educational arena. I'm not proud to admit it. But it's the truth. If I'm going to be successful, I must close that gap.

Most of the week, the fear of success and everything that comes along with it was crushing me.

Friday, that changed.

Following my "Quiet Time", I checked "Facebook."

A friend commented on a post: "You are such an inspiration. Success More Than Sleep."

I perked up and prepared for the day. The comment gave me the right energy. Also, it reminded me why I must close all the gaps in my life--personal, professional and spiritual.

I'm preparing my babies for the STAAR, have people who depend on me for encouragement, a future family that will need me to be their rock.

I leave you with two things.

1. What's your gap?
2. How can you close it?

God Bless, Jeremiah

01/29/17

Sunday's Reflection: "Be Mindful, Someone Is Watching"

As I took my "Walk With God", I thought about how someone is watching.

I've always been conscientious and mindful of my actions. A few years ago, though, it clicked that others watch what I do.

The Story

Before church, I usually grab a cup of coffee. Nothing major. One Sunday, I can't remember why, but I didn't grab that cup of coffee.

As I prepared to sit down, a church member, who sat behind me, said: "You don't have your cup of coffee?"

Me: Uh…

Made me think: If he notices that, what else to do others notice.

It's a thought process that I've carried into my role as a classroom teacher. Kids pay attention to everything that you do. They know your likes, dislikes and how you'll respond to situations.

This week, I realized that my kids were watching what I do.

Monday, I started off the week by showing my kids Eric Thomas' latest: "Dominate Your 1st Quarter."

In the video, ET tells the high school kids in attendance that they should start working toward their future now because it's going to be hard to catch up later in life--as there were adults in the room who weren't where they want to be in life because of decisions they made when they were 18 and 21-years old.

I talked to the kids about the video. I relayed to them: "I'm not where I'm supposed to be because I was lazy and didn't do the right things when I was 18 and 21."

Continuing: You're not even in the first quarter of your life. You're in pre-game…maybe even practice. You need to start now. I'm trying to make sure they don't end up like me.

It set the right tone for the week.

Wednesday, I reviewed for the upcoming Reading Checkpoint. I got upset, though, that they weren't focused enough.

I paused the video that I was showing them and let them know that they were "playing" and unfocused. I told them that they did well on their Reading Benchmark. 60 percent of them passed. But 60 percent isn't even average. If they didn't get it together, I wasn't going to put any more scores on the board until they reached 90 percent(Greatness).

They weren't going to slip on my watch. I don't believe in complacency.

Maybe they were listening. When I circled-up with the kids the next day, there was a cool moment.

I asked who studied for one hour. They looked at me like I was crazy. One hour…what's that?

I kept going up. Some kids studied up to six hours. One said that she was watching videos on her phone before she went to bed. Another said that she got up at 5 a.m. to study.

Obviously, she loves #successmorethansleep.

I was encouraged and proud of my babies. I found out that the checkpoint had been moved to the next week…bummed.

It didn't kill the day, though.

After grading a Campus Writing Assessment, I noticed that 80 percent of the kids passed. I made sure that the level of rigor was that of a checkpoint or benchmark. It was.

The kids had improved from 47 percent (nine percent above the school district) to 80 percent.

There was another cool moment that day. A co-teacher asked the kids: "How many of y'all read at home?"

Most of the kids raised their hand…too pumped.

Friday, I reviewed for the upcoming Math Checkpoint.

I reviewed decimals first. I started with converting fractions to decimals. It's a tough concept, except to one of my students, Rich.

He was flying through the worksheet that I gave him earlier in the day. I asked him what strategy he was using. He shared a strategy that his father taught him. I asked him could he show it to the rest of the class.

After he instructed on the strategy, the other kids grasped it immediately. I told him to show it to another classroom. When he returned to the classroom, I named him the "Student of the Week."

The other kids chanted his name. I joined in. He deserved to be exalted.

To end the day, I asked the kids how many hours of studying they were going to give me. Most of them said five or six hours.

I left the building knowing that I was modeling the right things to my kids.

I love to read. They love to read. I love to write. They love to write. I give 120. They give 120.

I'm striving for greatness. They're striving for greatness.

Be mindful, someone is watching.

I leave you with two things.

1. What are you modeling?
2. Is it the right thing?

God Bless, Jeremiah

02/05/17

Sunday's Reflection: "My Son, Calm Your Spirit"

As I took my "Walk With God", I thought about how I need to calm my spirit.

Monday, I woke up at 5:24 a.m. (not my usual 4 a.m.). I know, that's early. But my routine is my routine.

I couldn't get in The Word, mentally prepare myself, and I didn't get to work before 6:30. I felt like a bum.

The day went like the morning did…horribly. My kids didn't behave to expectation, instruction was average at best , and the kids scored poorly on their Math Checkpoint.

The next morning-- *The 21 Most Powerful Minutes In A Leader's Day*--posed a great question: Do you spend enough time listening to God?

While I pondered the question, a voice spoke to me: "My Son, Calm Your Spirit."

I didn't listen to it.

The day started off wrong again. The Uber that I requested drove to the incorrect location, there was a detour on the way to work, and my kids were acting like they lost their mind.

To end a messed-up day, the Reading Checkpoint was changed to an English/Language Arts Checkpoint…#TeacherLife.

This wasn't my week. I had a case of the Monday's and Tuesday's. I didn't know if I'd make it through it.

Wednesday morning, while searching for the Daily Word, I stumbled upon Mark 4:39: *"And he awoke and rebuked the wind and said to the sea, "Peace! Be still!" And the wind ceased, and there was a great CALM."*

I didn't heed the words.

I got upset while checking the scores for the ELA Checkpoint. That wasn't me.

When I got home, I self-assessed my behavior.

Thursday morning, I read Ecclesiastes 10:4: "If the anger of the ruler rises against you, do not leave your place, for CALMness will lay great offenses to rest."

My spirit calmed a little bit.

Following the sound advice of a mentor, I re-established the classroom expectations--for the kids and myself.

It seemed to make a difference. The kids were well-behaved, and the room's atmosphere relaxed.

Friday, the week ended on a high note. A work concern was addressed, the 100th day of school was celebrated, 14 kids volunteered for the Black History Month program, and I implemented a new writing strategy (I was happy with the results.).

After dismissal, I noticed a note that a student left on the board: "You can help us pass the STAAR. You're the Best Teacher Mr.Short."

Needed that.

Instead of bolting out the door, which I planned to do earlier in the week, I stayed late to organize and prepare for the next week.

As I reflected on the week, I answered that voice: Thank you God. I listened. My spirit is calm.

I leave you with two things.

1. Are you listening to God?
2. What is he telling you?

God Bless, Jeremiah

02/12/17

Sunday's Reflection: "Go To God First"

As I took my "Walk With God", I thought about how we need to go to God first.

Monday, I woke up at 4:34 a.m. The alarm didn't go off again…ahh. God doesn't waste any time seeing if you've learned your lesson.

Instead of day going poorly, it went smooth.

Tuesday, I had another good day.

The week was starting off on a positive note. When I got home, though, I received some troubling news. I didn't know how to process or respond to the information.

The next day, I was distracted. Instead of leaving my phone in "airplane mode", I had it on most of the day--waiting for updates on the situation.

At home, I contemplated: "How do I handle this situation?"

While contemplating, I remember the advice of a good friend, Robert Udoh: "Go to God first."

So, I asked God: "What should I do?"

The answer: "Realize what's important."

What's important? God, family and my babies. Everything else comes a distant fourth.

God sends those messages through many channels.

Thursday, one of the grammar lessons had an Aunt Flo, which is what my family called my Aunt Florence.

After the grammar lesson, I was given another reminder.

While my kids were sharing out their final drafts, I asked them questions about their revising and editing process.

One student: "I took out some sentences, because I realized it was off-topic."

Another student: "I realized that I forgot to put a word."

Third student: "I saw that I didn't punctuate."

I told them that they were starting to think like "Writers."

When I came to Thompson Elementary, my goal was to turn the kids into great writers. I have a few headed in that direction.

Later that day, I found out there would be a "Campus-Based Assessment." It was an opportunity to see if the kids were set up for success with the new Math instructional framework.

I called and emailed parents to make sure that the kids would study.

Friday, I found out that they did. 45 percent of the kids were Satisfactory (70). That's up 36 percent from the last checkpoint. If the Student Standard (STAAR Standard) was considered, 70-plus percent of them would have passed.

We celebrated by "Hitting Dem Folks."

I was excited for my kids. A few stick out to me.

Robert: I had to make a "failure" call to his mother earlier in the week. We discussed how he could improve his Math grade.

I needed more effort and focus from him.

Friday, he demonstrated that increased effort and focus. Not only did he pass, he showed his work.

Serena: Thursday night, she displayed why I consider her such a strong student. Her mother received my e-mail with the review material, but she wasn't at home. So, she looked it up on her own…lion mode.

She made a 78.

Jeffrey: He has struggled in Math. It hasn't deterred him. He works hard, doesn't complain and helps me lead his classmates. I told him to keep pushing. It would eventually show up.

Friday, it did. He passed. The first test he passed this year.

Before he left for the day, I had a quick word with him. I told him: "It's time to take it to the next level."

Even with the trials of life--personal, professional and spiritual-- moments like these remind me why we should "Go To God First."

He'll always have the answers.

I leave you with two things.

1. Do you go to God First?
2. If not, how would your life change if you did?

God Bless, Jeremiah

02/19/17

Sunday's Reflection: "Be Obsessed With Improvement"

As I took my "Walk With God", I thought about the classroom theme: "Be Obsessed With Improvement."

It wasn't just the theme but an expository topic, as well.

To set up the expository, I played Eric Thomas' "Be Obsessed With Improvement."

After playing the video, the kids wrote their rough draft. It's the first stage in my three-part writing process: rough draft, revising and editing and final draft.

Through that process, my kids displayed and learned the three components necessary for improvement.

1. Don't Subscribe To Someone Else's Standard

Monday, Marie, one of my talented writers, completed her rough draft, she asked me to read it. I did, and said it was a 4(Advanced).

The next day, while the kids were revising and editing, she challenged my opinion, saying: "Mr.Short, you said this was a 4, but I see a lot of mistakes."

She was holding her own standard. I loved it.

2. Give Up Stuff

Thursday, the kids shared their final draft. Michelle wrote that you must "give up stuff" if you want to go to the next level.

I couldn't believe it. One of my kids, a ten-year old, said that you must give up stuff. She's going to be ok in life.

3. Give Up Your Old Self

Thursday, while the kids were writing their final draft, Tracie was struggling to finish. I had a little conversation with her.

Me: "Why aren't you writing more? There's only one paragraph on that paper."

Tracie: "I can't think of anything to write."

Me: "You have plenty to talk about. You've improved more than anybody."

I got a little charged up at that point.

I continued, "You're not that kid anymore. So, stop thinking that way. There's nothing wrong with you. You're reading level improved. You did well on your test last week. Stop being that kid."

After our little talk, she completed her expository.

How did it turn out? She had one of the best papers.

I've experienced so much growth the past three years--personally, professionally and spiritually due to my own obsession with improvement.

I feel like the same person but a new person at the same time.

Personally, I've fought my untrustworthy nature and allowed people back into my life. There's a level I haven't reached yet. But I know I'll get there in time.

Professionally, I've grown. I was a paraprofessional who didn't know if he was coming or going most days. Now, I'm leading a classroom of kids.

Over the past six months, I've improved every day. I get excited thinking about where I'll be three months from now. I get even more excited thinking about where I'll be three years from now.

With the level of expertise at my school--fellow teachers, instructional coaches (Both kids scored 90 percent or above in their subject areas) and administrators, I might have the cheat code.

Spiritually, I grew when I first came to Christ, but I didn't take it to the next level until I started talking to God and asking what he wanted.

Because of my obsession with improvement, I have a balance that I didn't have for most of my life.

Be Obsessed With Improvement.

I leave you with two things.

1. Are you obsessed with improvement?
2. If you were, how would your life change?

God Bless, Jeremiah

02/26/17

Sunday's Reflection: "God Will Make You Look Like Him"

As I took my "Walk With God", I thought about how God will make you look like him.

This week, I was reminded of that.

Monday, I prepared the kids for the Writing Benchmark, but my Math instruction was interrupted by an issue.

Then after school, I was unprepared for two meetings. Not a good look.

Tuesday wasn't any better.

To start the day, I reviewed for the Writing Benchmark again. That went well. Math went poorly, though. The kids still weren't grasping the new concept.

After experiencing a few victories, I was facing a few challenges and roadblocks.

Should I complain? Should I sulk? Should I get bitter? Or Should I do what I normally do…get BETTER?

I had to remind myself: "Winners are fueled by the storm. When you come against them, present unnecessary obstacles or question their abilities, they'll show you how Great they are."

Self-assessing that night, I asked myself: How can you get better?

The answer: Become more prepared and get organized.

The next morning, I solicited my mother's help to organize my classroom.

On Thursday, we organized the room. It was eye-opening.

A moment sticks out to me.

While we were organizing the room, my mom saw some old student work.

She asked: "Are you going to use this for something? Are you going to give it back?"

Me: "No."

Her: "Then chunk it then."

It seems small, but that small conversation made me understand how disorganized my room had become.

Friday, a more organized room made a difference. After explained the new classroom rules, I had the kids organize their desk. Then we got to work. I broke down a reading passage with them. They were on-task, engaged and participating.

I can't take credit for the improved Reading Block, though.

Tuesday, my school's Literacy Coach, Mrs.Dixon, graciously modeled a lesson. Her energy level was off the charts. I had to match it.

She suggested that I change my groupings. I did that, as well. With that new information, my kids' reading comprehension and scores should increase.

Information does change situations.

During Math, my kids finally started to grasp using a protractor. That was a small victory.

The week was ending on a high note. My kids were well-behaved, engaged, and I was ready for Mannafest 2017.

Because an after-school training, I arrived late to Mannafest, though. I made it in time to hear the end of Blake Wilson's Breakout Session: "Transforming Men."

He said something that was deep: "When God sees an area in your life that doesn't look like him, he's going to make you look like him."

Throughout the duration of the conference, I marinated on his words.

When I arrived home Saturday evening, I had to ask myself some tough questions.

1. Am I the best employee? Not right now. I haven't been adequately prepared, steady or the leader that I pride myself on being.

2. Have I been the best friend? No. I don't reach out enough, and I dominate conversations.

3. Have I been the best Christian? No. I haven't been giving God the time he deserves. It's reflected in my Reflections. They've felt more like routine, instead of the inspired word of God.

I should have seen that my life was out of whack, though. I stopped doing the little things. I haven't been folding my clothes or keeping my apartment situated.

I stopped doing other things, as well.

I normally post articles to social media…daily. Lately, It's sporadic. I'm better than that.

Every Sunday, I assess my character and post it to social media. I'm still doing it, but it may get posted on Monday, not Sunday.

Every morning, I send the "Daily Word" to friends and family. For the past few months, I've gone days without doing it. That's not me.

I stopped looking like God. So, he put me through something to make me look like him.

I leave you with two things.

1. Does your life look like God?
2. If it doesn't, how could you start looking like him?

God Bless, Jeremiah

03/05/17

Sunday's Reflection: "The Light Will Come On"

As I took my "Walk With God", I thought about how the light will come on.

Wednesday, I was instructing on new concept (Supplementary Angles). It was proceeding well. The kids were grasping it. Then the lights went off. It got dark.

How did my class respond to the dark?

Before I tell you, let's backtrack to the previous week and lead up to the moment.

Last week, things got a little rough. It got dark. It was the first time that I questioned if I was on the right path.

When I went to sleep last Sunday, I was determined to have a great week.

The week started off right. I got in "The Word" and meditated on the ninth week of John C. Maxwell's "21 Most Powerful Minutes In A Leader's Day": The Law of Magnetism.

After my quiet time, I decided to check the Writing Benchmark scores. My kids didn't do as well as I'd like. I wanted to see their undeveloped strengths and strengths.

I saw that they needed to develop their revising skills. No shock. But I noticed something else: They did very well on their "expository."

A little breakdown.

18 percent of my kids scored advance (14 percent above the rest of the district). Then I saw that 73 percent of my kids scored basic (4) or above (20 percent above the rest of the school district).

I was so proud of my babies. They had come a long way.

At the beginning of the year, the kids had a Writing Checkpoint. Two kids scored basic or above. 16 scored basic or above on the Writing Benchmark…improvement.

That news gave me a bit of a boost.

To start the day, I talked to kids about the scores. I told them that we needed to improve on the revising and editing, but they did well on the writing. They didn't "dominate" (90 percent or above) the expository portion, but they have a chance to on the STAAR test.

It led into the theme for the week: "Don't Get Bitter, Get Better."

We started off the day getting better with a fellow grade-level teacher's class. They joined us for a writing session. It was fun. The kids were behaving, asking questions and having fun with the learning process.

That momentum carried into the Reading and Math block. 82 percent of the kids got their Math exit ticket correct.

Tuesday, the kids got 82 percent of their Complementary Angles exit ticket correct…consistency.

Wednesday, things got even better.

During planning, I was given an additional resource for revising and editing. Then I found out that Writing would be the primary subject taught the week before the STAAR test. I was hype. I'm about to "Go-Go Gadget."

I left planning pumped. The day proceeded, and the Math block came.

And then, that moment came. The lights went off. It got dark.

How did my class respond?

Initially, the kids were being a little silly. But I told them: "Stop acting silly. The lights are out, but you can still see the board. This is an opportunity to show how great you are. You're about to get 100 percent on your exit tickets in the dark."

So, we kept it moving. Eventually, the lights came on.

What percentage of the kids got their exit tickets right? 86 percent. They're close to greatness.

After school, I had another small victory. I successfully calibrated for TELPAS. It gives me confidence that I'll do well on my ESL (English Second Language) test.

Thursday, I instructed using the new resource for revising and editing. Everything flowed from the I/Do to the You(Do). My babies will be ready for that STAAR test.

Later in the day, we had, what was likely, the last "Creative Writing Club" session. So, I wrote an expository with them and model what great writing looks like.

Following Creative Writing Club, one of my school's veteran teachers, Mrs.Avington, gave me some tips on how to improve my classroom organization and overall repertoire.

She was like "change that", "this is good", and "it would be a good idea to do this."

All I could do was listen and take notes.

Friday, the kids had a "Pre-Benchmark." They didn't perform to expectation. We still have some work to do. I was determined to finish the week right, though.

After testing all day, the kids were a little rowdy. They did settle down to close the week with a writing lesson.

Before the kids left, I wanted to see if they understood the week's theme. So, I said: "The Greatness Room, we don't get bitter, we get what? "

And they responded (In Unison): "BETTER."

It was a great week. And after the darkness of the previous week, the light came on.

Reflecting, I didn't always respond to darkness the right way. It's crazy that it's been ten years since one of the darkest times in my life.

Heading into my senior year, I was backstabbed by some people, and I didn't understand why. It got real dark, and I wallowed in it. I was so stressed out that I lost 50 pounds, bombed most of my classes and blocked myself off from the rest of the world. I was darn near paranoid.

It wasn't like me. I never let stuff get to me. I wasn't raised that way. Weakness wasn't tolerated in either one of my families. You don't cry. You don't take "days." You keep it moving.

You darn sure don't trip over some beef with friends or a group of people that called themselves that.

And I had friends.

It's weird that I had a conversation with a childhood friend, Dezmond, about how we had a solid foundation from high school. We had friends. We never had to change or re-invent ourselves to gain new ones. We can still pick up the phone and talk to each other, even after several years.

Our squad was tight, too. Qyatis. Scutt. Moot. Dezmond. Fred. Mike. Steve. Bernard. A.D. I miss those boys.

I never should have tripped over what others had to say.

Here's why I couldn't deal with that situation, though: "I had a squad, but they weren't God."

I didn't have a spiritual foundation. I didn't believe in God. I identified as a Christian, but I wasn't one.

God used that situation, though, to shape me. That's how God operates. He believes in you, even when you don't believe in him.

I've grown since that time--as a person and Christian.

Example: There's a situation I talk about often. A girl from my church said that Black and Hispanic kids wouldn't ever be anything and others nodded in approval. I stewed on it for months, but I finally spoke up.

My stance had real consequences. I had several people coming against me. I stood firm. I went a step further and said that the ministry the person was a part of would destroy my church (I wish I hadn't said it that way.).

Things did get very "dark."

I remained steadfast and kept it moving. As my church started to push for a multi-cultural congregation, those people started to leave.

Last Saturday, I watched my pastor, Dr. Steve Bezner, talk to a room full of black men about his past experiences and thirst to have Houston Northwest look more like Houston(diverse).

If I had wallowed, instead of keeping it moving, I wouldn't have witnessed my church's light come on.

I leave you with two things.

1. How do you respond to the dark?

2. Do you wallow in it or do you wait for the light to come on?

God Bless, Jeremiah

Part V

Trust The Process

03/12/17

Sunday's Reflection: "Trust The..."

As I took my "Walk With God", I thought about my first big professional victory.

On Tuesday, there was a Math Checkpoint. It was the first Checkpoint since my grade-level started using a new framework for the subject.

After the test, the kids went to lunch and recess. The scores had come in, but I waited until the kids returned from recess to check them.

When they returned to the classroom, I logged in and viewed the scores. Then I recited the week's theme: Trust The...

And the kids responded: "Process!!!"

Me: "83(82.61) percent of y'all passed."

After I told the kids what they scored, we celebrated and celebrated some more. It was almost euphoric.

During the celebration, I called Robert's mother. I had contacted her earlier in the day, because he was having some behavioral issues. So, I figured she wasn't expecting good news and dramatized the moment.

Me: "I have some news (In a depressed voice)"

Her: "(Not saying anything but bracing herself)"

Me: "Your son made a 74."

The class started to chant his name. I can't find the words to describe the elation in her voice.

Once the kids settled, I gave them a writing assignment: a personal narrative of their favorite day. A few of the kids wrote that today was their favorite day.

The conclusion to Caroline's narrative was touching. She wrote: "I trust the process! I am great. That's why today was my favorite day."

While the kids were finishing up their narrative, the Math Coach came in the room and congratulated them. She told them that they had reached the school goal of 80 percent.

I interjected and said that it wasn't our goal, though. Then I asked the kids: "What is our goal?"

They screamed: "90 percent!!!"

The next morning, I told the kids that they were eight percent away from greatness. You see what happens when you get close to greatness. What do think will happen if you reach it?

I couldn't believe that I was having that conversation with the kids. Math had been a struggle all year. Only 45 percent of them passed the last Math Checkpoint. They improved by 37 percent...crazy.

While I was happy with the improvement in Math, I wasn't happy with the results of the UNRREAL--R&E strategy I had created a month earlier. Something in my gut told me to trust it, though.

That day, which was "Bring-A-Parent-2-School Day", I realized why the strategy hadn't yielded the proper results.

Following a "Revising and Editing" test, I checked the scores. The kids did well but not to my expectations.

Looking at the kids that failed, Arianna's name caught my attention. She had been doing well on her revising and editing assessments.

So, I looked at her test booklet, and saw that she didn't complete every step of the "R&E" process.

I asked her why she didn't.

She replied: "I forgot the steps. The anchor chart was up last time."

That let me know that the kids needed more reps. So, the next day I used two passages to re-teach the "R&E" process.

Friday, something unexpected happened.

After the kids listened to a few speakers for "Career Day", we worked through the Weekly STAAR Reading Passage. Once we worked through the passage, I gave the kids time to answer the questions. Then I graded it with them.

Half of the kids missed zero or one questions. I asked for feedback to find out the source of their improvement.

Listening to their feedback, I was shocked to hear several kids say the R&E strategy had helped them.

The strategy was created for Writing, but it was helping with Reading. It wasn't all luck, though.

Tracie said that the R&E strategy asks you to read the passage twice, and it helped her a lot.

It felt good to know that my kids were developing in every subject, and that I was finally getting in the groove of this teaching thing.

I told my kids to trust the process. I needed to take my own advice.

At the beginning of the year, I had no idea that I'd have an impact my first year.

That was furthest thing from my mind. I was more concerned with making it through a day. Now, it feels like I never have enough time.

I didn't know if I could reach my kids. The other day one of my kids left a note "thanking me for making her better in life."

I didn't know if I could help my kids improve academically.

Friday, the parent, who I called Tuesday, said that this may turn out to be the most rewarding year of her son's academic career.

That parent doesn't realize statements like she made are why this has been the most rewarding year of my life.

But that's because I trusted the process...God's process.

It's been a long one, too.

Recently, I heard a pastor talk about Joseph and what God had to put him through before he exalted him.

His process started when he was an arrogant 17-year-old and didn't reveal itself until he was a wiser, more mature 30-year-old.

I related to the sermon, because I've often wrote and told people that my life paralleled Joseph's.

I had dreams. I dreamed that my older sister, Christina, was pregnant, and that a child died. My sister ended up pregnant and a relative's child died (eerie but true).

I never prophesied my own greatness like Joseph, but others did. My Uncle Silas said I'd be smart. I was voted "Most Likely To Succeed." And my friends kept me out of trouble, because they thought I was destined to do something big.

I was never as arrogant as Joseph. But as I reflect, maybe I projected it.

I knew that I was intelligent. I could turn the switch on and off whenever I felt like it. The definition of arrogance.

Teachers and classmates would say things that fed into that arrogance.

I remember one comment from a classmate my Senior year. The classmate exhaustively stated: "Moot, nobody argues with you. They know everyone is going to agree with you anyway."

Me: "Oh, Word."

There were moments, though, where that arrogance was more pronounced. I remember a debate with a woman who was helping my Aunt Twanda at a catering event.

She told me that there's "Nothing New Under The Sun."

My precocious, arrogant response: "Things are different. We don't live in huts and stuff anymore." (Yea, I said that.)

We bantered back and forth. I can't believe how dumb I sounded.

Because of conversations like that, God knew I wasn't ready for what he had for me. He had to put me through a process before he released me for my mission.

He put me through a process in college to reveal my writing talent. Then he put me through a process after college to make me take that talent seriously. He put me through process that led me to him. Then he added kids to that process to make me step into my Greatness.

When I was 30 years old, after he put me through that process, he started revealing things to me.

I started to reflect. And through those reflections, I've started to help people with their own life journey by sharing mine.

The way people communicate with me is different than before. It's been surreal. People that I looked up to are looking up to me. I've had to catch myself from saying, "Why are you talking to me different? We're friends. You don't owe me that."

I respect them for respecting me, though.

That's why I must keep my eyes fixed ahead. That's why I must lead courageously, and why I must trust God's plan for my life.

We all need to trust it. So, say it with me, Trust The…

I leave you with two things.

1. Do you trust God?
2. If you did, how would your life change?

God Bless, Jeremiah

03/19/17

Sunday's Reflection: "Get You A Jonathan"

As I took my "Walk With God", I thought about how we all need a "Jonathan" in our life.

Who was Jonathan?

He was King David's, the second king of Israel, best friend. He wasn't a normal best friend. With all deference to "Rod" from "Get Out", he's the G.O.A.T. (Greatest of all Time) best friend.

Best friends are supposed to be encouraging, cool to kick it with and have your back.

Jonathan was all three and more. He was willing to go against his father--King Saul--the first king of Israel--in support of his friend.

When his father wanted to kill David, Jonathan advocated for him. When his father didn't heed the words, he told David where to hide.

Eventually, King Saul was killed, and David was anointed king. All because of the best friend who had something to gain from his death.

Think about that.

If Jonathan had allowed his father to kill David, he would have inherited the kingdom. He had faith in his friend and God, though.

During my quiet time, I meditated on week 11 of The 21 Most Powerful Minutes In A Leader's Day: "The Law of the Inner Circle."

The chapter made me think about the Jonathan's in my own life. I don't have many associates, but I have several friends.

Early in life, I was blessed with two great ones--Demetris and KO. I can't believe we've been friends for 20-plus years.

I had a great school crew, too. We're still friends. Love those guys.

As an adult, there are a couple of guys who have kept me sharp. Jamar. Cortez. Reggie. Dezmond.

My relationship with them developed in different ways.

Take Jamar or "Chaney" for example. He's the best natural leader out of that group.

Our relationship started off a bit adversarial. After I met him in the summer of 2008, we routinely debated about who should start at quarterback for Mississippi State.

People do that all the time, right?

Well…the problem is that I was a fan and Chaney was the actual "leader" of the team. It makes more sense now why he didn't care for me voicing my opinion on the matter.

The debate was settled, although I won't say who ended up being right.

After some initial friction, Chaney and I developed mutual respect.

I respected him more when he decided to coach high school football, instead of at the college or pro level. He could have done either. He was a college star and played a few years in the NFL. He was purposeful and intentional about working with that age group, though. He gave up money to follow his heart and passion.

Thanks Chaney for being a true leader.

Reggie is another friend who I respect. He has the best world view of all my friends. He's a darn good leader, too.

I've grown to appreciate our conversations.

Last week, he gave me info that confirmed that our friendship was ordained by God.

What was that info?

While we were talking, Reggie told me that his older brother was friends with my mom in school. Oh yea, my mom, Jeanette, was his teacher, too. Couple that with the fact that he was childhood friends with my older brother, Berto--and coached my baby brother--

Sammy, it's obvious that God wanted us in the same orbit until we became brothers in Christ.

No topic is off limits with him. Sports. Political. Financial. Personal. Spiritual.

The order doesn't matter. We might start a conversation talking about God, and then 20 minutes later we're talking about who should start at the "Will" Linebacker for "State."

During that conversation, there was another cool moment, which confirmed why he was my friend.

I was telling Reggie about a situation where I respected how a person responded to some direct words from me.

I told him that the other person has accomplished way more than me and could have dismissed what I said or got offended but didn't.

He responded: "That's emotional intelligence."

Then he explained in detail what emotional intelligence was and recommended a book: "Emotional Intelligence 2.0."

It's already on the bookshelf.

Thanks Reggie for the information.

I value Cortez, as well. I was connected to Chaney and Reggie through him. If you knew him, that wouldn't shock you. He's the definition of "the mutual friend."

He's gifted interpersonally. That may be an understatement. I'm convinced that he could make friends with a tree.

Cortez is gifted interpersonally, but I've grown to appreciate his directness, too. He'll hold you accountable and won't let slide when you're doing something out of step with God.

A conversation we had in 2014 comes to mind.

I was visiting Cortez and his wife for Thanksgiving. I was telling him about a situation, and how I was upset by it.

He deadpanned: "All I know with these situations is that you're the common denominator."

It was direct but true. I've evolved since that time, but I refer to that statement when I'm in danger of playing the blame game.

Thanks Cortez for being a real friend.

Dezmond is the most consistent of all my friends. He's the most consistent in his behavior and frequency in my life.

Often, I tell people that there aren't many people that understand me--even my family. The reason is that they haven't seen me through all my stages. Dezmond has.

That didn't hit me until this week. As I prepared to head to Atlanta (to serve as a groomsman is his wedding), I thought about how he has been there for every important point in my life: middle school, high school, college and adulthood.

We didn't begin as friends, but we were part of the same crew in middle school. In high school, we bonded over our mutual ambitious mindsets.

Our friendship has grown through the years--from college to adulthood.

That why I was honored when he asked me to stand beside him on his wedding day. That day was perfect, too.

No one in the wedding party wanted to mess up the special day. So, we worried that something would go wrong. But it never did.

A few of us were nervous about walking to the stage. That part went off without a hitch.

There was worry about spacing on the stage. There was plenty of space.

We worried that one of us would mess up the "Swag Surfin" intro planned for the reception. The intro was "live."

It was the most fun I've had since college.

The wedding almost served as high school/college reunion--as I caught up with a few old friends. That wouldn't have been possible without Dezmond. They were there to support him.

Showing up was their way of thanking him for his consistent friendship and loyalty.

I want to take time out to personal thank him, too.

Thanks Dez for being a true "Jonathan."

I leave you with two things.

1. Do you have a Jonathan in your life?
2. Are you the Jonathan?

God Bless, Jeremiah

03/26/17

Sunday's Reflection: "Create More Leaders, Not Followers"

As I took my "Walk With God", I thought about how we need to create more leaders, not followers.

Last Sunday, I returned from Atlanta, I headed to church and taught the children's lesson: "The Parable of the Vineyard Workers."

Following the lesson, the kids participated in an activity--acting out the parable.

Then I shared what Jesus said in Matthew 20:16: *"So the last will be first, and first last."*

After sharing the scripture, I asked the kids to interpret it. The kids collaborated to decipher the scripture. They weren't really used to it, so I had to "push" a bit.

Even after I pushed them, they still couldn't come up with the answer. So, I asked them to collaborate again.

Finally, after some more prodding, one of the kids said that no matter when we come to Christ, we'll all end up in heaven…boom.

It wasn't just a lesson for the kids but one for me, as well.

I realized that I needed to start training them to think for themselves and be leaders.

The same type of leaders that the kids I shepherd at school have become. They didn't get there overnight, though.

When the year began, I told my kids that I wanted them to be Great. Borrowing from some of the principles of Ron Clark and Eric Thomas--two great leaders, I created ten rules for Greatness.

For my kids to achieve that Greatness, they needed to take ownership of their behavior, not just the paying attention in class behavior but every behavior.

Example: Serena had a reputation as a bit of a "Drama Queen." She routinely overblew situations. I can never forget the day where she said that classmates had held her against her will. When I investigated, nothing of the sort happened.

Eventually, due to her Drama-Queen behavior, none of the other girls wanted to hang with her.

Taking all this into account, I had an adult conversation with her.

Me: "You claim that all your classmates are doing stuff to you, but then I hear reports of you cursing them out or writing stuff about them in your journal. Now, no one wants to hang with you. You need to look at what you're doing."

How did she respond to the conversation? She stopped being such a drama queen and has become one of my stronger students.

Another Example: I received a transfer student, Orlando, at the start the 3rd nine weeks. When his mom dropped him off, she asked to speak with me in the hall…uh oh.

She let me know that he was a behavior issue at his old school. I assured her that I'd get him right.

Immediately, he showed potential as a critical-thinker. It was confirmed when I looked up his test scores. Before he ran into the behavior issues, he was a high-performer. And when I say issues, I mean issues. He had been written up eleven times…yikes.

He regularly brought up that he had been written up on several occasions. I didn't see those negative traits, though. He was a good kid who had been "labeled."

After hearing him bring it up too many times, I told him: "That's over with…You're in "The Greatness Room" now."

How did he respond to the conversation? He's become a high-performer again--4 A's and a B in the 3rd nine weeks.

Those are individual examples, but I regularly have grown-up conversations with the whole class.

One day, after observing one of my kids fuss with her classmates, I told my students that when you get older, you're evaluated by bosses for your "ability to get along with others."

Their response: "For real."

Me: "Yep."

Through these conversations, I'm teaching my kids to "self-assess." They're not allowed to blame others for their mistakes. They must own them.

Once they started taking ownership of their behavior, I challenged them to take ownership of their learning. They had to study.

I was intentional about highlighting those who studied for Checkpoints. Before telling them the scores, I'd have the kids who studied stand up. Then I'd announce that all or most of them passed.

As my kids started taking ownership of their learning, the test scores started going up. At one point, my kids were 10 to 20 percent below their classmates in Math. On the last checkpoint, they scored nine percent above them. They literally went from last to first. I was told on Friday that the jump my kids made was…almost…impossible.

My babies are leading their classmates--literally and figuratively.

They displayed it this week.

To start "Camp-Write-A-Lot" (A week-long preparation for the Writing STAAR), we gathered all the kids for a pep talk.

I asked the kids to raise their hand if they had been studying for the test. About 25 percent of the kids raised their hands. My kids made up a lion share of the 25 percent, though.

They were being leaders.

Here's the cool thing: I asked the kids every day who was studying for the test. By Friday, most of the kids had started to study. At least 80 percent. I loved it.

There's a story within this story. During Camp-Write-A-Lot, I started to come into my "own."

I was empowered by Mrs.Dixon.

When we started preparations for the Writing STAAR, I wanted to try some different stuff with my kids. She's accomplished enough where she could just tell me do things her way, but she allowed me to experiment.

If something didn't work, she'd tell me why it didn't work and kept letting me do me.

She's pretty dope.

Wednesday, I found out how dope she was.

After I returned from taking my ESL (English Second Language) test, she was handling my rotation. When I walked in, I noticed the energy in the room. It was something that I'd never experienced.

She asked me if I wanted to take over.

Me: "Nah."

I wanted to be a student--a student of Greatness.

What do I do when I'm in the presence of Greatness? I take notes.

First Noticing: During the I(Do), she had the kids turned toward her. She explained to me why. I had to steal it.

Second Noticing: She had the kids wave their hands in the air when they got to the sentence that was being edited. I had to steal that, too. It increases engagement and taps a bit into the kinesthetic part of the learning process.

Last Noticing: She had the kids point to the word that they were reading. It's another informal way to check for engagement.

None of those things showcase her curriculum knowledge, but that's "on fleek", too.

She was the "Great Day Houston" Red Apple Award Winner in 2015. That means she was the best teacher in the city of Houston…Houston--one of the largest cities in America.

But even with those credentials, she let me be me. That's what Great leaders do.

They create more leaders, not followers.

I leave you with two things.

1. Are you a leader?
2. If so, are you creating more followers or leaders?

God Bless, Jeremiah

04/02/17

Sunday's Reflection: "I Can't Break My Promise"

As I took my "Walk With God", I thought how I can't break my promise.

After work on Friday, I went home, watched TV and tried to relax but couldn't. My spirit was disturbed. It was so disturbed that I sat up for 20 minutes…thinking. I was in a bad space.

At that moment, I'm thinking: Do I call someone? Do I text someone? Do I watch TV?

Instead of giving in to one of those mortal vices, I did what a Christian is supposed to do in moments of crisis: I had a talk with God.

Usually, I wait until Saturday morning to take my Walk With God, but something in my spirit told me to go have a conversation with him.

While I was on that walk, a voice came to me: "I can't break my promise."

It's a promise that I made early in the school year.

The Promise

One day, I was talking to the kids about Greatness and attached a numerical value to it. That number was 90 percent.

A student asked: "If 90 percent is Great, then what is 100 percent?"

Me: "Phenomenal. But y'all not ready for that. That takes a whole other level of focus."

I told them, though, that if they reached Greatness, then "The Greatness Room" would become "The Phenomenal Room" in the 5th Grade (I'm moving up a grade level with them.).

Monday, I put the kids through final preparations for the Writing STAAR, which was Tuesday, I told them that I passed my ESL (English Second Language) test.

Following that announcement, they clapped. I told them that I did my part to be with them next year...now they need to do their part tomorrow.

I didn't want them to just pass, though. In The Greatness Room, we don't compete, we dominate!!!

After the test (at recess), I found out that the kids wanted to meet that expectation. All my kids were saying that they studied for three hours-plus. That's after studying all spring break and over the weekend...Beast Mode!!!

One of my students tripped me out.

Student: "I forgot to study, but I worked on my writing."

Me:...

I wasn't too upset, though. That student has come a long way. At the beginning of the year, he was a major behavioral issue and folded paper--literally--most of the day.

Now, he's a minimal behavioral issue and actively participates in class.

Wednesday, I told my kids that I was proud of them. I demanded more, and they accepted the challenge.

Then I told them that they'd get a one-day break. After that break, it was go time again. I want them to score 90 percent in every subject.

Reflecting on that promise, my mind got back right.

Here's the mind trip: As humans, we struggle to keep promises for selfish reasons. Ego. Money. Pettiness.

We never stop, though, to think: God always keeps his promise to us.

His promise: If we give our life to him, then he'll give us eternal peace.

Here's the bigger mind trip: God doesn't need us and STILL keeps that promise.

Knowing that I need my babies, I can at least keep my promise to them.

I must teach them how to be Phenomenal.

I Can't Break My Promise.

I leave you with two things.

1. Have you made a promise?
2. Have you kept it?

God Bless, Jeremiah

04/09/17

Sunday's Reflection: "Get Tired Of Losing"

As I took my "Walk With God", I thought about how we have to "get tired of losing."

A conversation that I had with one of my kids made me realize it.

Thursday, after I announced the scores for the Reading Benchmark, one of my kids, Maya, was crying because she failed.

While the kids were at recess, I saw her sitting on the bench. So, I talked to her.

Me: We gave y'all the reading log. Do you read at home?

Student: Yes.

Me: Do you read 30 minutes or an hour?

Student: (Shook her head no)

Me: Well then…

I continued, "It's ok to cry for about 30 minutes. Let it out. Then get to work."

She wrote a note on the board thanking me for the talk.

Friday morning--inspired by that conversation--I decided to have a talk with the kids. I called it "The Greatness Talk."

The Greatness Talk

I started the talk by letting the kids know that 16 of them would have passed the Math Benchmark if they had correctly bubbled in their fill-in-the-blank questions. That's 76 percent.

I didn't stop there.

One student made a 40 and didn't even study. So, I asked him: Would you have done better if you studied?

He responded: Yes (Nodding)

There was another student who made a 45. He didn't study, either, claiming that the phone didn't work. (The classic dog-ate-my-homework excuse.)

I rebutted: "Your notebook doesn't work?" I know we've had checkpoints, and you've left your math notebook on your desk. You even left your Writing STAAR binder on your desk before Spring Break.

After that, I transitioned to talking about the Reading Benchmark.

To begin the discussion on the Reading Benchmark, I thanked the kids for doing what I asked.

What did I ask? I asked them to put a smile on Mrs.Dixon's face. She didn't have the best week.

I told them that she was happy with their improvement. And that's saying a lot. She holds the same high standard that I do.

I got serious, though. They improved but 61.9 percent wasn't good enough. That means 38.1 percent of them failed. I don't accept that.

I told them: No more writing stories or reading picture books for "When I'm Done" time. They needed to read. Not comic books or magazines but chapter books."

Following the talk on the Benchmarks, I shifted to a conversation on friends.

I highlighted two students. The students always bring up the fact that they go on play dates and hang out on weekends. One is a strong speller but struggles with reading comprehension. The other does well with reading comprehension but isn't a strong speller.

I asked: Why don't y'all help each other? That's what real friends do.

Then I highlighted two other students. They've both mentioned how they don't have anyone to help them at home with their studies. The two students "Facetime" with each other all the time.

So, I asked: "Why don't y'all Facetime and help each other study?"

At that point, I had a message for the kids who were upset that they failed the test.

I asked: If you failed, why are playing at recess? It's ok to play for about ten minutes. The rest of the time you need to be reading or studying your vocabulary words.

With all the talk about losing, I decided to share some more of my backstory with the kids. I told them that I worked security, but it wasn't very secure.

I brought up my last assignment as a security guard, which was only for a few months. After the assignment ended, I decided to quit.

The decision wasn't an easy one. I dealt with opposition from family. I was told that I was lazy, didn't want to work and all the other superlatives.

Also, I lived by myself and had bills. I couldn't pay those or rent. Eventually, I was evicted. That all led to a point where I was homeless for a day. It was one of the worst feelings of my life. But I wasn't just homeless because I didn't have anywhere to stay. I had a bad relationship with my sister at the time. So, I couldn't stay with her.

It was a tough situation, but I vowed: "Never Again."

I did get a job. Lost it. I kept on pushing, though. Then I got hired in education. Now, I'm here, and I knew I was meant to be here.

Why? I found out that a person, whom I struck up a friendship at my last assignment as a security guard, is good friends and college classmates with one of their classmate's dad.

Of course, they wondered which classmate. So, I told them.

Han opined: "Small World."

I let them know that she has improved more than anybody.

At that moment, I got emotional. I didn't cry, but I almost did.

Gathering myself, I kept with the talk on losing. I told them about my development as a writer. I started from the beginning. I was in Basic English my first year in college, because I didn't score high enough on a college-entrance test(A.C.T.).

Even as a college student, I still struggled. I would get a 100 for content and get marked down for grammar and punctuation. The same stuff they struggled with, but I was grown. They're in the 4th grade.

I struggled some more as I became a writer professionally. People clowned on me for my grammar...publicly.

Once people did that enough, I decided I was tired of losing. So, when my articles were published, I'd print out the edited version and compare it to my rough draft--identifying my grammatical errors.

Gradually, my grammar and punctuation improved. I wanted to take it to the next level, though.

So, I started sending my articles to national writers. They gave me critiques, which took my writing to another level.

I shifted my focus back to their Benchmark scores and brought up the theme of the week: "Don't Worry About They."

I told them that they say whatever you make on the Benchmark, then that's what you'll make on the STAAR.

Students started grumbling...

Then I deadpanned: "Who is They? I don't care about They. They don't matter. We're The Greatness Room. We're Great."

To end, I told them that chants are all good and stuff. But I didn't want them to talk about being Great. I wanted them to shh (finger on lips)...show me.

The speech was long (30 or more minutes) but necessary. I wanted my babies to understand Greatness and what it takes to reach it.

Throughout the day, the kids displayed a different level of focus. For example, as I reviewed vocabulary words and worked through a reading passage, they were energetic and engaged. I loved it.

Another example: Before the math lesson (Converting Measurements), I challenged the kids. I wanted 100 percent on the exit ticket.

What percentage of them got the exit ticket correct? 100 percent(Phenomenal).

Maybe they're ready to be Great.

Later that night, I was listening to a song "My Moment."

It was apropos. That song encapsulated everything that was my life in 2013. I was waiting on my moment.

Four years later, that moment has arrived.

All because I got tired of losing.

I leave you with two things.

1. Are you tired of losing?
2. If you are, how could start winning?

God Bless, Jeremiah

04/16/17

Sunday's Reflection: "Take Ownership For Your Life"

As I took my "Walk With God", I thought about how we must take ownership for our lives.

Wednesday, I was reminded of it.

I had a 30-minute lunch, but I needed some utensils. So, I went in the cafeteria to grab some. While I was grabbing the utensils, I saw one of my kids, Tony, sitting off to himself.

I asked him: "Why you sitting off to yourself?" (He didn't have silent lunch,)

His response: "They making too much noise." (Book in hand.)

My response: "Ok."

My response (In my head): *Shut yo mouth and keep on talking.*

I bragged on him all that day and the next. It represented a turning point for him.

During my "Greatness Talk", I challenged him to take more ownership. His grandparents don't always have the energy to work with him. I didn't know if the conversation resonated. But maybe it did.

The conversation seemed to hit home with his classmates, as well.

How do I know? They were focused all week.

Pushing for that 90 percent goal in Reading, I shifted the classroom instruction away from basic concepts to three main areas: mental stamina, skill work and word study. Not big stuff but sometimes less is more.

That same day, while doing sight words, I had a moment where I paused and beamed with pride at how hard my kids were working. I didn't have to re-direct anyone, and they were locked in.

Thursday morning, I told them: "I'm proud of the work you're putting in."

One of my students, Cameron, made me especially proud. He's my "Huck Finn."

For most of the year, this kid was dis-rup-tive. If you looked up disruptive in the dictionary, his picture might be there.

Over the past few weeks, he's shown growth. He's no longer disruptive but distracting. I wasn't satisfied with distracting, though.

Tuesday, I challenged him to take it to the next level. I wanted him to take more ownership.

I told him Greatness is more than not disrupting class. He had the potential to do better and needed to act like it.

The next day, he had his best day of the year. I only had to re-direct him once. And when the kids switched for Math Camp, I received a positive report from the Math Coach, who taught him during those two hours.

After-school, I relayed that news to his mother. She couldn't believe it.

Reflecting Thursday night, I had a surreal realization: I wasn't fussing at the student, but I was really fussing at a younger version of myself.

I was smart but did distracting things. I flat didn't care. Family members were frustrated with my ambivalent behavior. They thought I was too laid back.

They wanted me to be successful, but I didn't want that same success. I had the tools but didn't want it.

When I decided that I--Jeremiah LeShun Short--wanted to be successful, I stopped playing--figuratively and literally--and got serious about living up to my potential.

As I've stepped into a leadership role, I've learned that if you take ownership, then those you lead will take ownership, too.

So, I'm very purposeful, intentional and deliberate about letting my kids know that I take ownership for my failures.

My kids have experienced some success in Math, but I told them that the credit goes to the Math Coach, not me.

When the Literacy Coach modeled a lesson, she told the kids: Mr.Short told me that the knows how to teach Writing but doesn't quite know how to teach Reading."

I share my weaknesses with my kids to show them that it's ok to admit theirs.

It's a simple but Christian lesson: Take ownership for your life.

I leave you with two things.

1. Are you taking ownership for your life?
2. If you took ownership, how would your life change?

God Bless, Jeremiah

04/23/17

Sunday's Reflection: "We Stepped Into Our Rightful Place"

As I took my "Walk With God", I thought about how you have to step into your rightful place.

Tuesday, the kids had their first Math STAAR Prep assessment. They didn't score 80, 90 or 100 percent, but they improved from 43 to 52 percent pass rate. There were four kids one or two questions away from passing. That would have been 71 percent.

The improved Math scores created some momentum.

Thursday, the kids had their first Reading STAAR Prep. I was excited to see if they had improved since the Reading Benchmark. They were putting in so much work. I was hoping it paid off.

After the scores came in, it turns out that it did. If the STAAR Standard was considered, the kids improved from 61.9 percent to 67 percent. 52 percent of the kids made a satisfactory grade (Up 28 percent since the Benchmark). The class percentage was 61.10 percent--a five percent increase from the Benchmark (56.43 percent).

Friday, I highlighted the kids who improved and talked about why some had declined or stayed the same.

Two of the kids who improved the most might seem familiar.

Maya: Two weeks ago, I wrote that you should get tired of losing and used her as an example--telling her to cry for a little bit and then get to work.

Well...she got to work. That child improved from a 25 to a 57. With that score, she would have passed the STAAR. She passed her Math assessment, too.

Tony: Last week, I talked about how one of my students took ownership of his learning and started to read a book at lunch.

That child improved from a 31 to a 57.

After talking to the class about improvement, I talked about why some of their classmates declined or stayed the same.

I checked one of their classmates. He's one of my hardest workers and best kids, but he was lackadaisical about reading and wouldn't go the extra mile to build his reading level. He liked talking to his buddies.

I told him that he likes talking to one of his buddies at lunch, but his buddy passed the test. His buddy has time to talk, but he doesn't.

He needed to stop watching other people blow up. I told him that I'm a sportswriter and like to watch sports, but I don't watch the whole game. I watch the first and fourth quarter. In between those quarters, I read trying to find out how to blow myself and them up.

Then I turned it into a larger question for the class: "Are you willing to separate yourself?"

I meant figuratively and literally. I told them that it's not about being better than anybody. But if they wanted to take it to the next level, they would have to separate themselves.

I issued a challenge: Follow their classmate's lead and sit off to the side and read at lunch.

After that, I told them what the spirit had led me to say the night before: "Let's go for it."

Go for what? 100 percent on the STAAR in Reading.

Marie exclaimed… "Phenomenal."

A few hours later (on my lunch break), I walked into the cafeteria to check the temperature in the room. I looked over to the right and six kids were reading a book. I joined them and read a few pages of "Outliers."

I couldn't believe it. My kids were finally figuring out what it takes to be Great.

Friday night, I harkened again back to that girl saying that the Black and Hispanic kids she taught wouldn't amount much.

Last weekend, I told someone that they have no idea how it feels to be Black man and hear someone say something so vile.

I understand why God allowed me to hear the statement now, though. It serves as motivation for me as I teach mostly Black and Hispanic babies.

I did wonder, though, if I would push the kids who weren't Black and Hispanic.

But check this out. My highest-performer on the Reading test is Asian. Another Asian child failed most of her test last year. Now, she's making 70's and 80's.

I have one white student. I worried that I wasn't doing enough to push him.

A few weeks ago, his mother said that she was glad her son was placed in my room. It was such a confirmation--a confirmation that I was pushing all my kids, not just the ones who look like me.

I still pinch myself thinking about the impact that I'm having as a first-year teacher.

But I shouldn't pinch myself. It's what God ordained. He's the one directing my steps.

Not only is he directing my steps, but he's directing the steps of my family. We've come a long way.

I never thought we'd be in such a Great place. There was a time when I said that my family would miss our blessing. We were blessed with gifts but wasting them.

Don't get it twisted. My mom's generation made a few moves.

My Aunt Florence was an educator and people knew she was here.

My Aunt Sandra is a Spanish teacher.

My Aunt Twanda is a Postmaster and has a successful business: Southern Elite Catering.

My Aunt Allean also owns a successful business: Children's Escape Spa.

So, my generation saw a few people have success.

We were supposed to take the torch and run with it, but we didn't. We played around in school and weren't purposeful about our behavior. Our parents had us young and sacrificed their futures to raise us, and we were "playing."

A few years ago, my Aunt Florence passed away, and our mindsets started to change.

Walter, my Aunt Florence's son, made a wholesale change.

While hanging with some friends, he had an epiphany: What he was doing wasn't going to get it.

He started to engage in forward-progressing behavior. Now, he's a supervisor for "Best Buy."

A few weeks ago, his supply chain was awarded the "Center For Excellence." His distribution center is the top performing one in the company.

Even with the success of Walter, I don't think my generation would have taken it to another level if my brother, Roberto, and I didn't mend our relationship. We're the two oldest boys. We set the tone.

Our relationship was contentious for the better part of a decade. We agreed to disagree to keep the peace.

He's extroverted, and I'm introverted. We routinely brought it up in conversation that we were too different to get along.

During a conversation in 2014, I realized that we weren't that different. Berto was talking about how the people he supervised didn't like his direct style. People didn't care for my direct style, either.

We both wanted to grow. And we did.

Over two years later, Berto has been promoted to Master Sergeant in the Air Force. He's a "Hero of Texoma: MSG Roberto Short."

I'm a promising, young teacher and soon-to-be Author. (The book of Sunday Reflections is coming.)

Our relationship has been restored. I remember posting a Sunday Reflection and Berto told me that I was an inspiration. It hit me. I spent the better part of my life being jealous of him, and he considered me an inspiration. But he's an inspiration to me, too.

That's how it's supposed to be. We're only supposed to *outdo one another in showing honor.*

Reflecting on where our family is at now, I think of the next generation: Christopher, Cullen, Mason and Nicholas.

They're in a Great position. They have models for excellence and Greatness.

It's all possible because my family stepped into our rightful place.

I leave you with two things.

1. What is your rightful place?
2. Are you currently in it?

God Bless, Jeremiah

04/30/17

Sunday's Reflection: "They Reached Greatness"

As I took my "Walk With God", I thought about how my kids reached Greatness.

Monday, I went into the cafeteria to read with my "Greatness" Book Club. One more kid joined (Up to seven kids)

Tuesday, my kids took it to another level. When I went into the cafeteria to take them to the classroom for Book Club, my whole class decided to come back to classroom and read…yea!!!

While in the room, I read an excerpt from Relentless, a book I'm reading: *It doesn't matter what a Cleaner eats, he'll still be hungry again in an hour.*

My kids got the reference. I always tell them to be Lions, not Gazelles (The hunter, not the prey).

Wednesday, I told them the theme for the week: "It's Time."

Time for what? Time for them to step into their Greatness.

Thursday, they did.

Shortly before lunch, my kids finished their 2nd STAAR Prep assessment.

After transitioning them to the cafeteria, I went back to the room to have lunch. My lunch was interrupted, though, by Mrs.Gilley, the ESL Coordinator, banging on the window.

Her: "Dude, did you see your scores?"

Me: (Disheveled) What!!!? You are making me nervous.

Anxious, I opened my computer and checked the passing rate: Yes, Yes, Yes. One No. Yes, Yes, Yes…

Then I checked the overall pass rate…90 percent(Greatness). I darn near fainted. I couldn't believe it. My babies reached Greatness.

As my kids returned from lunch, I told them to hurry into the room. When they finally got in the room, I announced that 90 percent of them had passed. They reached Greatness.

I don't have the words to describe the excitement in the room. Maya was so excited that she cried.

We had to delay our celebration a bit. The other classrooms were still testing. After they concluded their testing, we celebrated our accomplishment.

During the celebration, I read another excerpt from Relentless: *Cleaners make the competition study them; they don't care whom they're facing, they know they can handle anyone.*

They were "Rock Stars" for a moment, but there was still work to do.

After the kids returned from recess, they got into "Stations" mode. I had two groups outside studying words, a few kids on the Chromebooks, and I was working with one of the kids who failed the test.

Of course, I was still planning on bragging, but I couldn't. Mrs.Dixon had already told everyone…like everyone.

This is how it went.

My kids scored 90 percent. Mrs.Dixon told me already.

My kids scored 90 percent. Mrs.Dixon told me already.

My kids scored 90 percent. I know, I was in the meeting Mrs.Dixon interrupted to tell everyone.

All I could do is laugh.

One person didn't know. My dad. I texted him the scores. He isn't the most tech-savvy (He just got a smart phone.). So, he asked me to call. I told him that 90 percent of my kids passed their test today.

His response was priceless: "All of them kids passed!!!"

My dad doesn't know what an emoji is, but he knows what 90 percent is.

Friday, I held a "Greatness" Party to celebrate my babies. While celebrating, I told my kids that they should celebrate for a minute, but that test wasn't the STAAR. We still have work to do and concepts to master.

The kids had a Math test. If they were going to score well, they needed to remain focused and not get to high on themselves.

If the Math test was any indication, they were a little high on themselves. Some of them didn't show their work and others didn't take the test serious. I was upset but glad at the same time. They needed a reality check.

I was proud of two of my babies, though.

1st child: Coming into the year, this child was struggling academically. She read at a level 24(second grade) and had a few deficiencies in Math.

This week, I was doing guided reading with her at a level 40(4th grade). She passed her Reading and Math test.

2nd child: Before the child transferred to my school at the end of the first nine weeks, she had developed "test anxiety."

After finding out that she had the issue, I started to build her confidence. Little by little, her nerves started to ease.

At one point, she wrote that she wasn't scared of test anymore. I asked why. She said that she "studied" now.

This week, she passed her Reading and Math test. Her mother was so happy. When I called Thursday to tell her that her daughter passed the Reading assessment, she exclaimed, "Thank You Jesus!!!"

After school, I was upset, though. I didn't like that my kids scored 90 percent in one subject but 50 percent in another. That's not Greatness.

It's the mindset that helped my kids reach 90 percent in Reading. I still remember teaching Reading early in the semester and not feeling it. I was teaching Reading but not TEACHING it.

Mrs.Dixon came in and modeled that lesson…game-changer. Something clicked for me.

Friday, someone mentioned how I had a "growth spurt." That's when it started.

After watching her, three things happened.

1. I defined my style.

Most of the year, I was unsure of how to maneuver in a classroom. Should I try to be technical or go get it? I knew what technical looked like, but I didn't know what go get it looked like. After watching her, I knew what go get it looked like.

So, what did I start doing? I started to "go get it."

2. I learned how to effectively use groupings.

After assessing the kids, Mrs.Dixon told me to change my groupings. I needed to match my stronger students with my weaker ones.

I made the changes. Those weaker student's scores started to increase.

3. I learned how to use classroom management to increase engagement.

After seeing Mrs.Dixon have the kids turn their chairs toward her for the I(Do) or instructional time, I started to do it.

But I took it a step further.

For the I(Do), I had a signal: Ooohhh….Woop!!!

To signal the We(Do) time, I say Boom while jumping in the air. Sometimes I even do twist. The kids loved it.

To signal the You(Do) or independent practice time, I say: All I know is…

The kids respond: You(Do)!!!

I've "come into my own."

If I had stayed in Cy-Fair, I don't know if that would have happened. I've been allowed to grow at my school and school district.

I still questioned at times why God sent me to my school, though. Then I thought about the response to my kids scoring 90 percent. The whole school was euphoric.

After disappointing STAAR scores, the school needed something Great to happen. The school needed hope that the ship would be righted. 90 percent communicates that.

The 90 percent encouraged parents.

Friday morning, two of my kids said that their parents were planning to transfer them to a higher-performing school. Now, they're going to stay.

If that's not God's hand, I don't know what is.

When God puts us on a mission, we must maintain a standard of excellence for him.

Before the year, I wrote that Christ wasn't in the school system, but he's in me. And I've taught my kids biblical principles without reading the Bible to them.

I tell them that they're Great every day. It's a metaphor for Blessed and Highly-Favored.

I always tell the kids to avoid distractions and remain focused. It's a metaphor for Proverbs 4:25: *Let your eyes look directly forward, and your gaze be straight before you.*

One of my 10 rules for Greatness is to honor your parents. My parents have helped me with the kids discipline and academics.

I tell them to always say Thank You (I got that one from Ron Clark). It's routine now for my kids to tell the cafeteria ladies Thank You when they come to pick up breakfast.

I asked them to study and work hard. It's a metaphor for Proverbs 21:5: *The plans of the diligent lead surely to abundance, but everyone who is hasty comes only to poverty.*

Finally, one of my core tenets is that you must be accountable.

Example: In last week's reflection, I wrote that I told Jeffrey to stop watching his friend blow up and blow himself up.

What did he do? He stopped watching his friend blow up. He jumped from a 38 to a 74 on his Reading test.

As a Christian, who is teaching my kids these principles, I must live it.

I tell my kids to avoid distractions. I had my car stolen at 6:30 p.m. and showed up the next day at 6:30 a.m.

I tell my kids to put others before themselves. I got rear ended heading to school on Awards Day. I still made it in time for the program.

I tell my kids to study and work hard. I get up at 4 a.m. and read when I get home.

As a result, They Reached Greatness.

I leave you with two things.

1. Are you ready to be Great?
2. Give your life to Christ and you will be.

God Bless, Jeremiah

The Epilogue

05/07/17

Sunday's Reflection: "Keep Your Eyes On The Prize"

As I took my "Walk With God", I thought about the theme of the week in my classroom: Keep Your Eyes On The Prize.

It was a message that my kids needed to hear. They did well on STAAR Prep 2, but it wasn't the STAAR test.

I didn't know that it would be so prescient and relevant to what they and I were about to face.

About an hour later (during my planning period), I pulled a few of my kids for skill work on the Chromebooks.

When my kids went to secure the technology, they were told that they couldn't have it. Upon hearing this information, I challenged the teacher on his behavior. We went back and forth, and then I told him that my kids would still "outscore" his. It didn't matter what he did (Not one of my finer moments).

The word that he called me in response was part wow and part…really?

Following PALM, I apologized to my kids for my behavior. They didn't need to see two adults arguing.

Shortly after that, my kids saw another classroom celebrating a good score. Then one of my kids asked: "Why when we get happy, someone come over. But when other people get happy, no one say anything."

I had no answer.

Sadly, my kids are learning, at way too early of an age, the price of success. You will have haters.

Comments have been made about them studying too much. They were called "distractions" for reading at lunch. And they were called "disrespectful" for celebrating their 90 percent score.

They've persevered despite the negativity.

During the Math Block, I realized why I need to keep my eyes on the prize.

While the kids were doing "drill and practice" on "Area and Perimeter", one of my students, Serena, started to cry because the concept was so difficult for her to grasp.

At that moment, I knew that I couldn't worry about foolishness. I had to put my focus back on my babies.

I was still a bit discouraged. Let me show you how awesome God is, though.

After-school, there was a staff training for the STAAR test. When the training was over, administrators gave kudos to the staff.

First, the Math Coach praised a few teachers for improved test scores on the final STAAR Prep Test.

Second, Mrs.Dixon gave her shout outs. She praised the 3rd Grade teachers. Most of them improved their scores from the first to second STAAR Prep assessments.

She got to the 4th grade. She announced that my team member improved from 50 to 80 percent from the 1st to 2nd STAAR Prep Test.

Then with a little pizzazz, she announced that my kids improved from 58 percent to 94 percent. The whole staff gave me a standing ovation. My mentor teacher stood up and said, "that's my mentee."

I was honored and appreciated the love. Leaving the meeting, a fellow teacher said that it was "inspiring."

The next morning, another teacher called me "Mr.90 percent." I chuckled and told her that my kids need to do it on the STAAR.

It was a solid instructional day--as my kids comprehended a difficult concept: Strip Diagram.

Wednesday, a co-worker said that they almost cried when someone read last week's Sunday Reflection: "Be A Cleaner For Christ" to them.

Thursday, there was another Reading assessment on two tough concepts: Paired Passages and Poetry.

The scores weren't expected to be good, and they weren't. Only about half of the kids passed. I took solace in the fact that 48 percent of the kids made a Satisfactory (70) grade and the rest were on the bubble.

After the test, I had the kids clean out their desk and help me prepare the room for the STAAR.

One of my kids left a card on my desk.

It read: "We achieved Greatness because of you. We can beat anyone! :)"

At recess later, the same child approached me--with a serious/sneaky look-and asked: "You really think we're going to score well on the STAAR?"

Me: "Yea."

Friday, shortly before planning, I tested one of my kid's fluency. She read 227 words per minute (20 words above 6th grade). The kids were hype. It set a good tone.

After PALM, I gave the kids a practice Math test to model how they should properly show their work.

It was enlightening. I saw a few bad habits. One child--showing his work--wrote: "process of elimination." I told him to work the problem again. After missing it the first time, he got it correct.

Modeling good testing habits must have worked. 83 percent of the kids passed. It was only ten questions on difficult concepts, but I was encouraged.

Before the kids left, I had to pump them up a bit. I told them that it was ShowTime. Then I proceeded to say: We don't compete, We…

They responded: Dominate!!!

They did that three times. Then I said: "We're…"

They responded: "Great!!!"

I switched it up for the last chant. Instead of saying We're Great, I told the kids to chant "We're Phenomenal."

I could feel the energy in the room. My babies are ready to rock the STAAR.

Reflecting on the week, I learned a few lessons.

1. Tame Your Tongue.

Death and life come from it. Jesus says it in Matthew 15:11; *"It is not what goes into the mouth that defiles a person, but what comes out of the mouth; this defiles a person."*

2. Haters Gonna Hate And You Can't Stop Them From Doing It.

In Proverbs 27:4, it says so: *"Wrath is cruel, anger is overwhelming, but who can stand before jealousy?"*

3. Love Your Enemies

I'll share a scripture from the prayer book a parent gave me on Friday: "Prayers for Difficult Times."

You shall love your neighbor and hate your enemy. But I say to you, love your enemies and pray for those who persecute you, so that you may be sons of your Father who is in Heaven.

When facing opposition and trials, remember to "keep your eyes on the prize."

I leave you with two things.

1. Are you facing opposition?
2. Despite that opposition, are you keeping your eyes on the prize?

God Bless, Jeremiah

05/14/17

Sunday's Reflection: "What I Do It For"

As I took my "Walk With God", I thought about what I do it for.

Wednesday evening), it became clear when I had my kids write a reflection on the school year.

Afterwards, they shared their reflections with the class. They were touching and insightful.

Let me paraphrase a few.

Orlando: Following trouble at his old school, he transferred to Thompson and came to the so called "Greatness Room."

They were having a pizza party for a good score. He didn't accept a pizza, because he didn't feel he deserved it.

But soon, he became one of the most successful students, met new friends and didn't fail any test.

He ended by saying that he had a great year. How about yours?

Felicia: She started her reflection off by saying that her school year was great because she had a teacher who pushed her to be better at reading.

She wrote about how she didn't talk much at the beginning of the year. But she started to and earned an S for conduct, instead of an E. To go with the talking, her attitude started to come in, and she got in trouble for it.

After writing about her struggles, she wrote that we made 83 percent in Math and 90 percent in Reading.

Michael: This student's reflection isn't about what he wrote. …It's more about how the class helped him share it.

I asked this student to share his reflection, but he experienced some stage fright. I told him that I'd read it with him. He still had some trouble. So, I asked his classmates to read along with us. They did.

After we read the reflection together, the other kids encouraged and clapped for him. It immediately became one of my top 5 moments of the year.

Reflecting on their reflections, I shared my reflection of the year from the teacher's viewpoint.

I shared that I was scared at the beginning of the year. I didn't know how I'd make it through the day.

Then there was a lot of classroom disruption. It was tough as a teacher to deal with it. I wanted them to succeed academically, but I didn't want them to feel "unsafe" in my classroom.

They were in an unsafe classroom and weren't succeeding academically. There were a few tests where 10 to 20 percent of them were passing. Then someone told me to model studying if I wanted them to study properly.

Once they started to study properly, their performance started to improve. It improved so much that they did well on their Benchmarks. They went from the worst-performing classroom on the grade-level to the best.

I was worried, though.

People were praising me. I thought that others would hate on me. I've dealt with it throughout my life.

I pushed past that, but I was too tough on them during the 3rd nine weeks. I was taking things they didn't know about out on them.

At that moment, I apologized for that behavior.

Then I talked about how great a feeling it was for them to score 82 percent in Math and 90 percent in Reading.

Also, I didn't know yet if I'd get to show them what Phenomenal looks like, but I know I had helped them reach Greatness.

The week wasn't done. I had a few more things to share with the kids.

Friday, while they were composing the final draft of their reflections, I played an audio from Eric Thomas, which I had been marinated on the past two weeks.

He spoke about what every person should have in them.

After the audio concluded, I left them with a simple message: "If there's anything you learn from me this year, it's that you should never get comfortable with losing."

Later that day, I realized that they weren't.

Before the kids left, something told me to do the "We're Great" chant.

I said: "We're"

Instead of saying Great, they responded: Phenomenal!!!

I loved it.

Greatness means someone will lose. Phenomenal means that no one loses. They're ready to go to the next level.

Chants are Great, but my main goal for the year was to have my kids take ownership of their learning and lives.

Friday night, I read Han's, who didn't share in front of the class, reflection and realized that he did take ownership.

It was so good that I must share the whole thing.

…on next page

My 2016-2017 School Year

At the start of the school year, I was bad. So, I had bad reports, a few phone calls home, and I was lazy.

I slowly started to behave, and I got good conduct reports, and my mom was happy. When I started to behave better, my grades went up.

I started talking more, but I still got good reports. But they sometimes come with "notes."

It took a long time to prepare for STAAR, but then "Ms.Dixon" and Mr.Short helped us pass. We had study plans and Greatness hour. So, I think we will pass.

Short but terrific reflection on the school year. It captured everything that I want a student to be in my classroom.

I want them to self-assess, honor others, improve behaviorally and academically.

That's' what I do it for.

I leave you with three things from one of my students.

1. Never Give Up
2. Try Your Best
3. Be Phenomenal

God Bless, Jeremiah

05/21/17

Sunday's Reflection: "Going To The Next Level"

As I took my "Walk With God", I thought about going to the next level.

Tuesday, the grade-level assignments for next year were e-mailed to the staff. I've come to understand that it's akin to the NBA Draft Lottery--everyone waiting to see where they'll be slotted.

I was drafted to the 5th Grade team. It's the move that I wanted for two reasons.

1. I wanted my kids to have a complete Mr.Short the whole year. I was still trying to keep my head above water the first half of the year. The second half of the year I started to figure it out. Imagine what my babies could do if I knew what I was doing from day one.

2. I wanted to be a part of a strong team. And it is.

Check out this line-up: The Rookie of the Year, a Teacher of the Year finalist, a former Teacher of the Year and "Mr.90 percent."

It's the teaching version of a "Super Team." Maybe I'm engaging in hyperbole...Maybe not.

Ironically, right before the assignments were e-mailed, Michelle--in response to observing my competitive nature during "Field Day"--asked: "What if we have a teacher like you in 5th Grade?"

Me: That'd be crazy, huh? (Knowing I was likely moving up with them.)

30 minutes later, I announced that I'd be moving up with them. They were excited. Their parents were, too.

One parent e-mailed: "Yaaayyyy!!!!!!!!!"

I was saying Yaaayyyy, too.

My kids worked on their weekly expository: "What I'm looking forward to next year?"

Most of them wrote about how they were excited to have me as a teacher again next year and looking forward to becoming Phenomenal (100 percent).

Friday, I delivered the "Phenomenal Talk."

It wasn't particularly deep, but I did let the kids know what I wanted from each of them if they were to become phenomenal.

After the talk, we went outside for the grade-level picnic. My parents came through--figuratively and literally.

I didn't buy any materials for the picnic. So, one parent purchased snacks, drinks and brought a tent. Another parent bought drinks.

While the kids enjoyed the picnic, I figured it was a good time for them to sign "The Greatness Room" plaque--seeing as it will become "The Phenomenal Room" plaque next year.

Next year will be special, but I faced some challenges and struggles to make it through this one.

My team dynamic was rough and could best be described as "toxic."

I was on an island.

God was testing me. He put through a similar test my first year in education. People were praising me--saying that I had potential to be a great teacher. Then I started getting bullied by veteran teachers.

Instead of rising above their negativity, I let them get to me.

This year, when God sent similar challenges my way, I let the negativity fuel me.

During the same week that my vehicle was stolen, I was told that my "scores weren't looking good."

The next week, the scores started looking good.

At one point, I was told that I wasn't prepared enough, needed to get my stuff together and couldn't help my team, because I didn't have the data.

Shortly afterwards, 82 percent of my kids passed their Math Checkpoint(Data), even the "bad kids" passed (At least that's what one of my kids said).

For "Writing Camp", I was asked to teach the most difficult concept(Revision). To go along with teaching the most difficult concept, I was asked to work with the bubble writers—since I was the "Best Writing Teacher."

Following the second round of Benchmarks, I was told not worry about the non-bubble kids. I challenged my kids to step it up, and they did. They started reading more, even while being called "distractions" for reading at lunch.

Their reading scores increased on the first STAAR Prep and peaked on STAAR Prep 2…90 percent(Greatness).

God put me through the storm. Now, he's putting me where he needs me to be--on a Great team.

The team has the credentials and superlatives, but I'm most excited about the intangibles of it.

We're all emotionally intelligent, embrace unity and want to push each other.

Iron does sharpen Iron.

We will darn sure keep each other sharp.

With that team dynamic, the most important people in the equation will benefit: the kids.

If the kids don't pass the 5th grade STAAR tests, they're not promoted to the 6th grade. So, we must be a strong team. It's the only way our kids will be "set up for success."

Thursday, I realized that things would be different next year.

While I was getting to know my new team, I mentioned how I wasn't going to do my tutorial payment forms since they were a little cumbersome.

Then one of my teammates offered to help. It was kind…of…refreshing.

All I could do is thank God.

I'm going to the next level.

I leave you with two things.

1. Are you ready to go to the next level?
2. If you put your faith in God, you will.

God Bless, Jeremiah

Conclusion : I Started To "Fly"

As I took my "Walk With God", I thought about how I started to "fly."

Last year, during a Children's Ministry meeting, the interim pastor, Stacie Barron, praised me for my work with the kids and gave me my own classroom. (I was an assistant the previous two years.)

She ended her praise with a prophetic statement: "It's time for you to 'fly'."

It was a figurative statement, but it ended up being literal and allegorical.

It was literal because I took a flight to Mexico for my second mission trip--representing Team USA in the World University Championship--that Friday, which was a life-changing experience.

Coming at the midway point of the trip, I didn't get a chance to know everyone. But as the journalist, I got to share the testimonies of Vattel Voight, C.J. Grice, Reggie Langford and Matt Davis.

C.J. is still pursuing a professional career. Reggie blogs and is playing football overseas. Matt was the Division II Special Teams Player of the Year.

I had an opportunity to develop a relationship with the two chaplains--Willie "Chap" Templeton and Steve Debardelaben.

I roomed with Chap. I'm still impressed by his faithful and humble demeanor.

Pastor Steve was quite humble, too. He could easily act big time. He was the chaplain for some big names at Miami--"The U."

Ray Lewis and "The Rock" come to mind.

We were connected through another name: Cyrus McGowan.

Cyrus is my younger cousin who played basketball at The U. He met with Pastor Steve when my Aunt Florence was battling cancer the first time.

How crazy is it that two kids from little ole Brooksville, Mississippi would end up connected with such an influential person?

The relationships that I built and experience in Mexico prepared me for my next mission: teacher.

I was scared but excited to teach Writing. That excitement only lasted so long--as I found out during trainings that I'd be teaching all five subjects: Social Studies, Writing, Reading, Math and Science.

That wasn't what I signed up for.

I don't question God, though. He sent me to my school.

How do I know?

During the same week that Stacie told me that it was time to fly, I interviewed for my current position. My principal told me that they're eagles at Thompson...eagles soar(fly).

Before I was offered the job, I knew Thompson was where I wanted to be. God had already confirmed it.

That didn't mean teaching wouldn't be a challenge. I didn't even know what the theme of my room would be.

Then one day, someone did a presentation on the Urban Learner. It was informative and inspiring.

I learned that the biggest indicators for the success of the Urban learner is parent involvement and homework.

After one of the presenters told the teachers to "be yourself", I was inspired.

I reflected: How can I be myself?

It hit me. I love Greatness. I'll call my room "The Greatness Room."

I didn't understand the tone it would set. When I told the parents that the theme of the year was "Be Great", they loved it. The kids loved it even more. They wrote the word Great everywhere. It was in their spirit.

I was motivating my kids, but I wasn't doing a good job of teaching them. People still thought I had potential. One parent even went so far as to say that I would be a "superstar."

I didn't even get it. Had she seen my kids' scores?

After a rough start, though, my kids started to improve. The apprehension started to dissipate, as well. I started to enjoy teaching.

Then "STAAR Season" came. I developed tunnel vision. My only focus was preparing the kids to dominate the STAAR Writing, Math and Reading test.

While I didn't manage the stress that comes along with the STAAR well, I did a good job of preparing my kids for their assessments. I'll know for sure in a few weeks.

As a teacher, you're judged off your kids' academic performance, but I wanted my kids to grow as people, too. And they did.

They learned what "off-topic" and "redundant" were from me. But they also learned how to be Great.

In addition to learning how to be Great, my kids learned other things. They would even quote me.

Two examples.

1. Early in the year, one of my kids was upset that I didn't praise her for getting the answer right.

Her classmate interjected: "Don't expect affirmation."

I loved it.

2. Two weeks ago, my kids were doing a group project. After seeing one of her classmates trying to complete it too quick, my student opined: "Don't rush the process."

I was hype.

That child wants her classmates to succeed. She thinks they're "Lit, Phenomenal Winners." (Yea, my kids be doing too much.)

My kids listen to me, though, because I lead by example. I don't tell them to do anything that I wouldn't do.

Example.

Wednesday, while we were heading to our field trip location, I took the time to look at the 5th grade Math curriculum. (My kids struggled in Math this year. That's not happening again.)

Jeffrey saw me looking at the material and said: "Look at Mr.Short studying."

But check this out.

The next day, Tracie received her "Summer Reading Plan", she asked: "Can I take a break from learning?"

Me: "Nah."

I have the right to tell her that, because I don't take a break from learning. I read at least five books a month--hoping to learn some nugget that can help me improve myself and the others around me.

Moments like those make realize that I've found my lane. I've become a "change agent."

I've Started To Fly.

Acknowledgements

I had a successful Rookie Year. I didn't do it on my own.

My family helped me. They gave me "The Blueprint."

My mentors--Bill Buckley, Allen Tate and Dobie Weise—helped me. I've learned so much from them.

They're not the mentors many would expect me to have. They're all older, white males. I don't write that to say, "I friends with a white person." I write it to say that true Christianity doesn't have a color.

I have mentors but "My Boys" keep me sharp. I'm blessed to have Jamar, Cortez, Reggie and Dezmond in my life.

My day ones--KO and Demetris--have helped me.

KO kept me out of trouble because he thought I had a chance to do something. He saw something in me when I didn't see something in myself.

Demetris was always there for me when I needed to vent. He heard about all my losses. Now, he's happy to hear about my victories. That's a true friend. There for the ups and downs.

My Carlton Center fam helped me. I became a man there. They wanted me to be successful and equipped me with the tools to do so.

I became a man while at The Carlton, but I stepped into my Greatness this year at Thompson.

A few of my co-workers truly helped me become Great.

Mr. Neblett, my mentor teacher, was the perfect model. The kids even called me the new Mr. Neblett. Our mentors were chosen for us, but I wanted him to be my mentor. I saw the way he carried himself and how the other teachers responded to him.

In my mind, I thought: "He's Great. I want to learn from him."

He taught me so much. Tracking data. Classroom management. Professional responsibilities.

I respected that he knew me. One day sticks out to me. He told that I tend to "over talk" sometimes. I need to get comfortable with the silence.

I was like, dang. That's why I over talk, because I don't like the silence. Most people think I do it because I want to "dominate the conversation."

Mrs. Avington, my unofficial mentor, was awesome, as well. She allowed me to vent when there was an issue. She did something else, too. Through watching her, I learned how a Christian teacher is supposed to act. She's tough but loving.

My co-workers must have felt the same way about her. She was voted "Teacher of the Year."

Mrs. Scott is the best. She was always there to check me when I was being "frustrating" or acting "foolish," which is most of the time. (I'm the worst about turning stuff in on time.)

The funny part is that she'll say it in such a way that you end up agreeing.

Her: "Mr. Short, you do some frustrating stuff."

Me (with a smile): "Yea, I can be a little frustrating."

Ms. Dixon is the embodiment of Greatness. When I found out that 95 percent of her kids passed the STAAR Reading test, I knew I had to learn from her.

While learning about the academic side of teaching from her, I realized that we clicked the same.

She called her classroom the "Genius Zone." I called mine The Greatness Room. She bought her kids gifts. I buy my kids gifts.

Sharing a similar mentality, she knew where I was coming from. When others thought I was upset no reason, she knew I was frustrated and for the right reason.

Her support allowed me grow…to fly.

Ms. Day, our assistant principal, is a jewel. We had a disagreement or two at the beginning of the year. After that, she became one of my biggest champions.

She kept me calm when was getting worked up. She helped me with classroom management. She also was quick to check me when I was running my mouth too much.

She'd say: "Mr. Short, that's extra commentary."

I'll never forget that conversation we had with a parent. She told the parent that if she needed a mentor for her son, he was in the room.

That student, who had trouble at several schools, got his behavior together by the end of the year.

On the last day of school, before he got in his mom's vehicle, he gave me a hug. If it wasn't for Mrs. Day, I don't know if that would have happened.

Thanks Mrs. Day.

My parent-educators were a godsend. They disciplined their kids if they got out of line and made them do their homework.

My babies gave me a reason to show up. They're my why.

I cherish those small moments with them.

Serena, when entering the room, like clockwork, would say: "Good Morning Mr.Short."

I looked forward to those words.

As Caroline rode off, I would always wave goodbye and dab in unison with her.

There was nothing better than the notes my kids left on the white board. They kept me encouraged.

My babies, my why, are why I could conquer my demons, which is why I was able to start flying.

I never forgot about who got me here…God. He was there with me the whole time. Not figuratively but literally. I kept a Gideon's bible on my desk. I never opened it. I never moved it. But I knew I was "covered."

God has had me covered through every step of my journey. I don't know where he'll send me to next.

But I know I'll be flying.

God Bless, Jeremiah

www.ingramcontent.com/pod-product-compliance
Lightning Source LLC
Chambersburg PA
CBHW051841090426
42736CB00011B/1911